The
Portable
English
Workbook

The Portable English Workbook

William Herman

*The City College of the City
University of New York*

Holt, Rinehart and Winston
New York   Chicago   San Francisco   Philadelphia
Montreal   Toronto   London   Sydney
Tokyo   Mexico City   Rio de Janiero   Madrid

To my son, James,
who is very fond of books

ISBN: 0-03-059423-5

Copyright © 1982 by CBS College Publishing
Address correspondence to:
383 Madison Avenue
New York, N.Y. 10017

Printed in the United States of America
Published simultaneously in Canada
8 9 10 059 10 9 8 7 6 5 4 3

CBS COLLEGE PUBLISHING
Holt, Rinehart and Winston
The Dryden Press
Saunders College Publishing

Preface

The Portable English Workbook has been designed with utility in mind. It begins with a basic grammar and covers virtually all areas of grammatical and rhetorical problems as well as the techniques involved in writing effective sentences and paragraphs. Tests are provided at the end of each section to help the student measure his or her success in particular subjects. The book concludes with a pretest and a posttest to measure the gains the student has made over the whole subject.

The instructor is in the best position to decide how the book should be used, but I should make clear that it can be used either in conjunction with *The Portable English Handbook*, 2nd ed. (the Contents is referenced to relevant sections of that book), with another handbook, or simply on its own: the material in the headnotes to the exercises is ample for that.

Exercises are plentiful and can be done either in class or at home. Wherever possible, they have been structured to require students to write—not just make choices or change something that is wrong.

Many possible writing assignments will be found in Part 4, "Effective Paragraphs and Compositions." The section contains numerous paragraph assignments and many possible topic sentences. This section also contains checklists to help the student rewrite and proofread.

Diction covers a good deal of important ground designed to sharpen the student's awareness of slang, specific diction, wordiness, idioms, and vocabulary building. The last section offers a positive program for the acquisition of new words.

Spelling also offers a positive program for improvement and brief but pertinent exercises and headnotes.

I should like to acknowledge once again the elegant assistance of my colleague, Professor Edward Quinn. I also wish to thank my editors at Holt: Susan Katz, Anne Boynton-Trigg, Nedah Abbott, and Kenney Withers. Professor Richard Beal's comments at various stages of the manuscript were invaluable, and my son James Paul Herman must also be mentioned: he drove me mercilessly to completion.

W. H.

Contents

Basic Grammar

1 Parts of Speech: Nouns

Nouns are the names of persons, places, things, ideas, qualities.

Characteristics of Nouns

1. Nouns can change form (be *inflected*) to indicate either the plural or the possessive.

apple—*apples*   Danny—*Danny's*
table—*tables*   friend—*friend's*

2. Nouns can be preceded by small words like *a, an, the, each, my, this, that,* and so forth. Nouns can also be preceded by another possessive noun.

the lake   *Judy's* ceramics   *each* morning
a boy   *Jo's* telephone   *that* cake
an orange

3. Nouns occupy certain positions in the sentence: subject, object, object of a preposition, indirect object, object complement, predicate noun, appositive.

Subject   The *toast* is burning.
Object   She threw the *ball*.
Object of a Preposition   He walked *to* the *car*.
Indirect Object   We gave the *cat* some milk.
Object Complement   They called him a *fool*.
Predicate Noun   He is a *policeman*.
Appositive   My Uncle Sam, the *coach*, made me a quarterback.

4. Nouns are sometimes formed by adding suffixes either to nouns or to adjectives or verbs.

king + *dom* = *kingdom*   consider + *ation* = *consideration*
deny + *al* = *denial*   young + *ster* = *youngster*

5. Nouns are divided into special classes to describe them further:

A. *Simple and Compound Nouns.* A simple noun is one word: *tree, hat, horse;* a compound noun consists of more than one—usually two—words: *shoestore, menswear, salesperson, boardwalk.*

B. *Proper and Common Nouns.* A proper noun is the name of a particular person, thing, place. Proper nouns are always capitalized, except for those articles, prepositions, and conjunctions that are not the first word of the group: *the World Trade Center, Dallas, The Jeffersons, The King of England, the Fourth of July, Jill Clayburgh.* A common noun is any noun that is not a proper noun: *building, hall, window, bike.*

C. *Countable and Mass Nouns.* A countable noun has both a singular and plural and is able to be counted: *chicken/chickens, car/cars, penny/pennies.* A mass noun has no plural form, cannot be counted in units, and is not ordinarily used with *a* or *an: sugar, magic, atmosphere.*

D. *Abstract and Concrete Nouns.* A concrete noun names something that can be grasped with the senses: *velvet, dog, fog, skyscraper.* It may be either a countable or a mass noun. An abstract noun, usually a mass noun, names something intangible—an idea, a concept, a quality: *tenderness, democracy, imagination, psychoanalysis.*

E. *Collective Nouns.* A collective noun names a group of people or things: *herd, jury, team, audience.*

---

1 Exercise/IDENTIFYING NOUNS

Underline *all* the nouns in the following sentences.

1. Martha keeps a pet cougar near her bed.
2. The dream I had this morning featured an old trunk, my math teacher, Professor Buckley, and a gold coin.
3. Charley bought his jalopy in a junkyard and now he keeps it in his backyard.
4. Football is probably America's favorite sport.
5. Although inflation worries rich people, it probably has a greater effect on poor people.
6. At the lake, we fished, swam, and sunned ourselves; then we made dinner and sat around singing songs all night.
7. Math exams take the heart out of me.
8. Women with minds are very attractive.
9. Everybody has imagination to some degree.
10. Some people say that magic is a form of superstition.
11. The newspapers are so full of warnings about how dangerous to the health certain foods are that I hardly know what to eat.

4

12. The <u>hand</u> is quicker than the <u>eye</u>—if the eye is closed.
13. Paris is the <u>city of light</u>.
14. Travel is more than <u>mere entertainment</u>.
15. The <u>social life on this campus</u> is too meager.

2 Parts of Speech: Verbs and Auxiliaries

A *verb* describes action or a state of being.

Characteristics of Verbs

1. Verbs have three principal parts:

Infinitive   to play   to feel
Past Tense   played   felt
Past Participle   played   felt

2. Verbs change form to indicate a change of time (tense). Using the principal parts shown above and various auxiliary (or helping) verbs, combinations can be made to alter the tense of verbs.

Present Tense   Joanna *watches* the baby.
Past Tense   Joanna *watched* the baby.
Future   Joanna *will watch* the baby.
Perfect   Joanna *has watched* the baby.
Present Progressive   Joanna *is watching* the baby.

3. Nearly all verbs have an *-ing* form. All verbs of the present tense, indicative mood, end in the letter *-s*. Many verbs change to their past tense forms by adding *-d* or *-ed*. (See below, number 7, for what is meant by indicative mood.)

-ing Forms   jumping, skipping, flying
Third. Pers. Sing. Forms   is, has, goes, helps, plays
Past Forms   waited, needed, wanted, watched, peeped, prayed

4. Verbs can be single words (*sings, worked, touched*) or they can consist of several words (*has gone, will be promoted, should have been asked*). *Has, will, be, should,* and *have* are all *auxiliary* or *helping* verbs. (See below for more on this type.)

5. Verbs are the most important parts of the predicate of the sentence. That is, we can divide all sentences into two parts, a subject and a predicate. The subject is usually a noun or a pronoun, and the predicate must always contain a verb, although it can also have some other parts of speech:

6

```
subj.  v.    pred.
```
Birds *sing* sweetly.

George *should have been elected* mayor last year.

v.

6. Verbs have a property called *voice* which indicates whether the subject of the verb performs or undergoes the action. When the verb is in the *active voice*, the subject is performing; when it is in the *passive voice*, the subject is being acted upon.

Active John *ate* the rabbit. Jose *saw* the president.
Passive John *was eaten* by the rabbit. Jose *was seen* by the president.

7. Verbs also have a feature called *mood*, to indicate the manner in which they are used: The *indicative mood* is used for statements of fact or other kinds of assertions or questions; the *imperative mood* is used in issuing commands or giving directions; the *subjunctive mood* is used for statements contrary to fact or those that are in the area of possibility or potential.

I *gave* him a tennis ball. (Indicative.)
Can you *lend* me ten dollars? (Question—also indicative.)
Give me a Cadillac. (Imperative, a command.)
Turn left at the red light. (Imperative, a direction.)
If I *were* you, I'd buy the Toyota. (Subjunctive; the speaker "I" is not "you.")

8. Verbs fall into two classes: *linking verbs* and *action verbs*. Linking verbs are all forms of the verb *to be: is, am, was were,* and so forth, as well as such other verbs as *feel, seem, become, appear.* Linking verbs are so called because they *link* the subject to another noun or pronoun or an adjective and thus describe the subject's state of being.

Frank *felt* anxious.   Uncle Al *seemed* quiet.
You *are* beautiful.   Eddie *is* a dancer.

Action verbs describe what is happening—an action. They can be further divided into *transitive* and *intransitive* verbs. A transitive verb describes action that is received by something; the *something* is called the *direct object* of the verb.

Jim Plunkett *throws* the *ball.*
Gravity *moves* the *planets.*
Women *date men.*

Intransitive verbs also describe action but they do not act *upon* something but merely describe the action performed by the subject.

Christmas trees *burn* easily.
This typewriter really *works.*

But some verbs work both transitively and intransitively. Notice what we can do to the two verbs just used as examples:

The stove *burns* coal. (Now it's transitive.)
John *works* the farm.

An *auxiliary* is used in combination with verbs. Some are used by themselves.

Characteristics of Auxiliaries

1. Auxiliaries have different meanings and change the meanings of verbs they couple with. For example, they indicate time and therefore change tense:

She *was playing.* She *had been playing.*

A subgroup of auxiliaries called *modals* (*should, would, could, can, may, might, must, ought to, have to, shall, will*) add meanings that suggest possibility, ability, obligation, and so forth.

She *must play.* She *might play.* She *can play.*

Notice that these modals are always used with the present tense stem of the verb.

2. Auxiliaries are widely used in asking questions.

Shall we go? *Did* you play? *Must* you sing? *Should* he drive?

3. Only forms of the auxiliary *be* appear with verbs ending in *-ing*.

I *was* jumping. They *were* jumping. He has *been* jumping.

4. Forms of *be* and *have* are used with past participles such as *known, played, gone, remembered.*

I *have known* him. I *was known.* She *had remembered.*

5. The auxiliaries *be* (*am, is, are, was, were*), *have* (*has, had*), *do* (*did, does*), and *can* can also be used as verbs. We see this when one of them is used so as not to be followed by a verb.

Do as an Auxiliary   Sarah *does listen.* (*Listen* is a verb.)
Do as a Verb   Sarah *does* laundry. (*Laundry* is a noun.)

2 Exercise/IDENTIFYING VERBS AND AUXILIARIES

A. Which words in each of the following sentences denote action and which denote state of being or condition? Write your answer in the blank space provided. Some sentences have more than one verb.

Example   She removed her shoes. __action – removed__

1. Harry felt lonely. __action – felt__

2. Tom threw a party. __action – threw__

3. The committee elected a chairman. __action – elected__

4. My mother cried and my sister seemed sad. __action – seemed, cried__

5. I love to visit the city, but after awhile I become anxious there.
__action – anxious, to visit__

B. Find the word in the following sentences that can be changed to indicate a change of time. Then write in the blank space provided a different tense of the verb.

Example   My father had played basketball. __is playing__

1. He has been working as a longshoreman. __is working__

2. They never serve wine at dinner. __never served__

3. They will be married on Sunday. __they'ed be__

4. I am going to the beach. __I went to__

5. He was riding his bicycle. __he had__

C. Over each auxiliary verb in the sentences below, place the letters AUX; over each verb, place the letter V.

1. He was washing the dishes while she was solving math problems.

2. Because they were visiting their parents and had neglected to close the windows in their apartment, the rain has ruined the rug.

3. He would close his eyes and think of the woods around the lake; only that way could he get to sleep.

4. I must remember to make a deposit in my savings account by the tenth; otherwise, I will be losing interest.

5. They have known each other so long that neither has ever failed to remember the other's birthday.

D. Over each linking verb in the sentences below, place the letters LK; over each action verb, place the letters ACT.

1. She seemed graceful.

2. They drove cattle.

3. Wendy shortened the hem of her dress.

4. Al became a father.

5. When they were happy, they often enjoyed a picnic lunch on the sundeck.

3 Parts of Speech: Adjectives

Adjectives are words that further identify nouns or complete the sense of a linking verb.

The *sad* mouse   The *mouse* is *sad*.

Characteristics of Adjectives

1. Adjectives change form to compare two or more objects. This can be done by adding *-er* to the basic adjective (a form called the *positive*) to make the *comparative*, and the ending *-est* to the positive to make the *superlative*.

Positive	Comparative	Superlative
happy	happier	happiest
young	younger	youngest

However, some adjectives form the comparative and superlative by adding the words *more* and *most*.

Positive	Comparative	Superlative
beautiful	more beautiful	most beautiful
honest	more honest	most honest
recent	more recent	most recent

Also, some adjectives form the comparative and superlative in an irregular manner.

Positive	Comparative	Superlative
good	better	best
bad	worse	worst
many	more	most

The comparative form is used to compare two objects.

He is *happier* than I am.
His home is *more beautiful* than mine.

The superlative is used to compare more than two objects.

I am the *happiest* man in the whole world.
That is the *most beautiful* table I've ever seen.

2. Many adjectives have characteristic endings that can help you identify them. Here are a few:

-al (accidental, international)
-ant, -ent (resistant, excellent)
-able, -ible (comfortable, irresistible)
-ar, -ary (solar, ordinary)
-ful (careful, wonderful)
-ish (boyish, sluggish)
-ive (attentive)
-ous (generous)
-y (funny, sloppy)

3. Many different kinds of words function in sentences as adjectives.

My cat is a hero. (The pronoun *my* = adjective.)
His hair is red. (*His*, the possessive, is also an adjective here.)
He is *that* kind of person. (The demonstrative *that* = adjective.)
Which road should we take? (Interrogative *which* = adjective.)
The ball is round. (The article is an adjective.)
We lost in the *fourth* quarter. (Numbers can also be adjectives.)

---

3 Exercise/IDENTIFYING AND USING ADJECTIVES

A. On the line below each sentence, copy out all the adjectives you can find in that sentence.

1. The long day came to a beautiful end.

_____

2. Before he could manage to buy a new house, he had to pay off his old debts.

_____

3. There was something strange about that man.

_____

4. She was much happier than I.

_____

5. Whenever we had a good long talk together, we felt better.

_____

6. Which road should we take?

_____

7. His Chevrolet was an ordinary car but to him it seemed to have a special quality.

_____

8. Pure water is essential if we are to have a clean environment.

_____

9. Certain songs always remind us of happy moments in our lives.

_____

10. It was a stormy day, but a piece of blue sky could be seen beyond the threatening clouds.

_____

11. Lost and frightened children always arouse our deepest sympathy.

_____

12. Many Americans are sick over the increased rate of inflation.

_____

13. He had a boyish look about him but he was older than you might think.

_____

14. We had an excellent meal at a small, waterfront café, and then we took a comfortable stroll around the town.

_____

15. She did careful laboratory work; thus when she broke the test tube, we knew it was accidental.

_____

16. The driveway took a sweeping curve up the green cottage and then disappeared into the gray afternoon.

   _____

17. The incidental music to the play was lively and at the same time sweet and warm.

   _____

18. The sluggish fish swam in slow circles.

   _____

19. The brutal math exam given by Professor Greene ruined a beautiful grade-point average.

   _____

20. A friendly Irishman is an irresistible companion.

   _____

   B. Write sentences using adjectives according to the specifications given.

   Example   (using the comparative form of *happy* to modify the noun *mood*)

   I was in a happier mood than she.

   1. (using the superlative form of *bad* to modify the noun *violinist*)

   _____

   2. (using the comparative form of *thankful*)

   _____

   3. (using the superlative form of *recent* to modify the noun *incident*)

   _____

   4. (using the comparative form of *evil*)

   _____

5. (using the superlative form of *handsome* to modify the noun *carpet*)

_____

6. (using the comparative form of *severe*)

_____

7. (using the superlative form of *trusting*)

_____

8. (using the comparative form of *dreary* to modify the noun *day*)

_____

9. (using the superlative form of *modest* to modify the noun *writer*)

_____

10. (using the comparative form of the adjective *clean*)

_____

4 Parts of Speech: Adverbs

Adverbs are words that modify the meaning of a verb, an adjective, or another adverb.

Characteristics of Adverbs

1. Adverbs in sentences express several different kinds of modification.

Manner   The airplane rose *gracefully*.
Time   We will play tennis *today*.
Place   We will eat dinner *there*.
Degree   The soup was *very* good.
Negation   We were *not* hungry.

2. Some adverbs are identical with prepositions.

He drove *up*.   She walked *by*.   They ran *on*.

3. A few adverbs, like adjectives, can change form to compare qualities or degrees by adding the endings *-er* and *-est*.

Positive	Comparative	Superlative
soon	sooner	soonest
quick	quicker	quickest

However, most adverbs form the comparative and superlative by adding the words *more* and *most*.

Positive	Comparative	Superlative
often	more often	most often
rapidly	more rapidly	most rapidly

A few adverbs form the comparative and superlative irregularly.

Positive	Comparative	Superlative
badly	worse	worst
well	better	best

4. Adverbs occupy certain typical positions in the sentence.

She drove *in*.   She was lucky *rarely*.
She drove *seldom*.   She was lucky *often*.
She drove *perfectly*.   She was lucky *there*.

5. Adverbs can often be moved from one position in the sentence to another without changing the meaning of the sentence. This flexibility is in contrast to adjectives, which must remain relatively fixed if the sentence is to retain its meaning. In the following example, *lucky* is the adjective and *often* the adverb. Notice that we *can* alter the position of *often*.

Often, she was lucky.
She was lucky often.
She was often lucky.
She often was lucky.

Now try moving *lucky* the way we have done with *often*. What are your results?

6. Adverbs frequently end in the suffix *-ly*, and many adverbs can be formed by adding this suffix to an adjective.

Adjectives	Adverbs
rapid	rapidly
sweet	sweetly
tense	tensely

The difficulty is that no all words ending in *-ly* are adverbs. Some nouns add *-ly* to form *adjectives*. (But some adjectives ending in *-ly* are *not* formed from nouns, for example, *unsightly* and *unlikely*.)

Noun	Adjective
beast	beastly
brother	brotherly
earth	earthly
king	kingly
love	lovely
heaven	heavenly
man	manly

---

4 Exercise/IDENTIFYING AND USING ADVERBS

A. Underline all the adverbs you find in each of the following sentences.

1. Usually, he could swim fast, but today he had a cramp in his leg and he went slowly through the water.
2. He rarely had the nerve to stand up to the bully on his block, but now he was determined to fight manfully for his rights.
3. She danced gracefully, although her partner was painfully clumsy.
4. The wind blew frigidly across the mountain ridges.
5. The stove was very hot.

6. Then Dick sang; he began beautifully, but he faltered badly at the end of the song.
7. Arthur clunked noisily up the stairs, muttering angrily under his breath.
8. She drove up to the house, the car skidding wildly as its wheels slipped in the dry roadbed.
9. He was rather afraid of his father, but he and his mother got along very well, indeed.
10. The road was temporarily impassable because of the heavy rains that had fallen there.
11. He was completely drained of energy because he had danced unceasingly all through the night.
12. Normally he would have taken it more easily, but the music stirred him up.
13. Tomorrow, when he would be better able to judge, he would decide; clearly, he was in no condition to do so today.
14. He moved rapidly from city to city, anxiously looking for a job, never finding one suitable enough.
15. He worked best under pressure.

   B. Write sentences fulfilling the specifications given.

   1. (using *hard* as an adjective)

   _____

   _____

   2. (using *hard* as an adverb)

   _____

   _____

   3. (using *fast* as an adverb)

   _____

   _____

   4. (using *fast* as an adjective)

   _____

   _____

5. (using *good* as an adjective)

_____

_____

6. (using *well* as an adverb)

_____

_____

7. (using *badly* as an adverb)

_____

_____

8. (using *quick* as an adjective)

_____

_____

9. (using *quick* as an adverb)

_____

_____

10. (using *more* as an adverb)

_____

_____

5 Parts of Speech: Prepositions

Prepositions are used to connect a noun or a pronoun with other parts of the sentence.

Characteristics of Prepositions

1. Prepositions are used to form phrases, called *prepositional phrases*, which begin with a preposition and are followed by a determiner (a word like *a*, *an*, *the*, *this*, etc.) and then a noun or a pronoun. Sometimes the determiner is not present. The noun in the phrase is called the *object of the preposition*.

prep. obj.
from California
to my *house*
above the *door*

Some of the many English one-word prepositions are the following: *aboard, against, along, at, between, before, by, for, from, in, of, to, up, upon, with, within.*

In addition to these, a number of prepositions consist of more than one word: *ahead of, as well as, away from, by way of, in back of, in place of, in spite of, on account of, up to.*

2. The word *to* used in the infinitive form of the verb—for example, *to play, to dream, to love*—is not a preposition.

---

5 Exercise/IDENTIFYING PREPOSITIONS; USING PREPOSITIONS TO MAKE PREPOSITIONAL PHRASES

A. Underline the prepositions in each of the following sentences.

1. They ran to the store where they went from stall to stall buying all the fresh fruits and vegetables on display.

2. Under the roof, the gutters dripped rain onto the already muddy ground.

3. To my father and to my Uncle William, I owe my love of learning.
4. With my gloved hand, I reached through the broken glass in the window and unhooked the catch.
5. Down the road came the horse and buggy and behind them a troop of children, singing.
6. Throughout the hotel, the news spread that the rates would rise on the following day.
7. Across the road, he saw a horse beside a bale of hay.
8. Among the students, Professor Quinn's reputation is very high.
9. Inside the building, he spotted a man in a blue uniform and walked toward him to ask for information.
10. He threw a light raincoat over his shoulders and dashed out into the rain.

   B. Select twenty of the prepositions previously listed, and using the following list of nouns and a determiner where needed, construct twenty prepositional phrases.

Nouns: farm, apple, newspaper, pizza, automobile, ferry, chair, horse, tomato, road, chopsticks, burglary, television set, stadium, football field, day, California, France, camp, lake, moon, room, cage, planet.

	prep.	d	noun
Example	beyond		the planet.

6 Parts of Speech: Conjunctions

Conjunctions act to join together words, groups of words, or even whole sentences. There are three main types: *coordinating conjunctions*, *conjunctive adverbs*, and *subordinating conjunctions*.

Coordinating Conjunctions

This group consists of the seven words *and, or, but, yet, for, nor,* and *so.* They are used to connect elements of the sentence that have the same functions. For example, they can connect two subjects, two objects, or two independent clauses. *So, for,* and *nor* (without its accompanying word *neither*) link together clauses only.

Apples *and* peaches are delicious. (Links two subjects.)
I bought a red Ford *and* a green Mustang. (Links two objects.)
My father likes to play tennis *or* to fish on his vacations. (Links together two infinitive phrases here used as objects.)
We were discouraged by the rain, *for* we had no umbrella. (Links two independent clauses.)
The dime in the meter did not register, *nor* could we find out why. (Links two independent clauses.)
She took her exams with enthusiasm, *but* she failed them all with F's. (Links two independent clauses.)
He had no money for train fare, *so* he decided to hitchhike. (Links two independent clauses.)
She had very little money, *yet* she always seemed well dressed. (Links independent clauses.)

But is commonly used to join pairs of adjectives or adverbs that are somewhat opposed to each other in meaning.

He was poor *but* happy.
She looked quickly *but* carefully.

Correlative conjunctions are special types of coordinating conjunctions, occurring only in pairs.

both ... and   not only ... but (also)
either ... or   such ... as
neither ... nor

22

Conjunctive Adverbs

This group of words acts to connect independent clauses—like the coordinating conjunctions—but unlike them it does not always appear at the *beginning* of a clause; sometimes it appears within the clause.

He had graduated with honors; *therefore,* his chances for graduate school were excellent. (Conjunctive adverb begins the clause, has a semicolon to its left and is followed by a comma.)

He had graduated with honors; his chances for graduate school were, *therefore,* excellent. (Conjunctive adverb within the clause is set off by commas.)

He had graduated with honors. Therefore, his chances for graduate school were excellent. (Conjunctive adverb begins the clause but also begins the sentence. It has a period preceding it and a comma following.)

Some of the conjunctive adverbs are the following, with their meanings in parentheses: *for instance, for example, namely* (illustration); *however, nevertheless* (contrast); *furthermore, moreover, in addition, also* (addition); *then, thereafter, consequently* (time); *therefore, consequently* (result).

Note: When you join two independent clauses with a conjunctive adverb, you must use either a period or a semicolon. If you use only a comma, your sentence will be a comma splice.

Subordinating Conjunctions

Subordinating conjunctions are used to join a subordinate clause to an independent clause. The subordinate clause is made subordinate by the presence of the subordinating conjunction; without it, the clause would be independent.

I made a deposit in my account. (Independent clause.)

When I made a deposit in my account. (Dependent or subordinate clause, made so by the word *when,* a subordinating conjunction.)

Subordinating conjunctions appear in subordinate clauses that begin a sentence or end one.

Because its engineering school is excellent, I selected M.I.T.
I selected M.I.T. *because its engineering school is excellent.*

Here are some subordinating conjunctions:

after	provided	whatever
although	since	when
as	that	whenever
because	though	where
before	unless	wherever
if	until	whether
lest	what	while

6 Exercise/WORKING WITH CONJUNCTIONS

A. Describe your routine this morning—from the moment you awoke until you arrived in your English class. As you write, construct sentences that will include at least *four different coordinating conjunctions, three different conjunctive adverbs,* and *three different subordinating conjunctions.*

B. Underline all the conjunctions you find in the following two paragraphs.

1. Although many Americans are unaware of it, many of us are overweight and the reasons have to do with our ordinary physical routines. More and more of us work at sedentary occupations; therefore, more and more of us get less exercise and consequently do less work to burn the rich caloric intake of our diets. These diets consist of more carbohydrates, sugars, and fatty meats than we need. Although the recent increase in our exercise patterns—jogging, karate, tennis, and the like—are partly responsible for a narrowing of the gap between intake and burn-off, we nevertheless need to do more. For the pace of modern life, say experts, has much to do with persuading us to eat more junk food, too, and these foods contribute to our overweight problem.

2. When inflation is high and unemployment is used to dampen its effects, students are likely to be most affected because they hold part-time jobs, in the main, and these kinds of jobs are the first to decrease in number. Therefore, students who want part-time work need to be very aggressive in going after jobs. They need to explore every avenue of possible employment; they can consult newspapers and they can write letters of application, but personal visits are even better. Because there are many applicants, students need to put their best feet forward, so to speak, and these feet should be well shod. Dress is very important, but so is a well-documented résumé that tells an employer what the student can *do* for him. In short, when employment opportunities are low, a student must *work* to get a job.

7 The Grammar of the Sentence

An English sentence does two things: It names something and it says something about the thing it has named. What is named is called the *subject*, and what is said about it is called the *predicate*. Every predicate has in it at least one finite verb (that is, a verb other than the infinitive form—for example, *to play*, *to drive*—or the *-ing* form). A sentence is also called an independent clause, and we cannot easily define a sentence except to say that it is a variant of one of seven basic patterns.

Something Named (Subject)	Something Said About It (Predicate)
Dogs	bark.
Fish	swim.

To find the subject of any sentence, first find the verb and then ask the question of the verb, "who?"

In the above examples, looking at the verb *bark*, we ask "who barks"? The answer is "dogs," the subject.

PATTERN 1: Subject (noun or pronoun) + Intransitive Verb

An intransitive verb is one that does not have to act *on* something but only reflects back and describes the action performed by the subject.

subj.	intr. verb	subj.	intr. verb	subj.	intr. verb
He	smiled.	Birds	sing.	The doors	closed.

We said that these are basic patterns, which means that the pattern can be expanded.

Looking around at the crowd, *he smiled* slowly and sweetly.
Birds who are well fed *sing* all day long and far into the night.
With a great crashing noise *the doors closed* on the prisoner.

The portions of the expanded sentences not italicized are modifiers.

Who *smiled*? "He," the subject. Who *sings*? "Birds," the subject. What *closed*? "Doors," the subject.

PATTERN 2: Subject (noun or pronoun) + Linking Verb
+ Predicate Adjective

In this pattern, the predicate adjective completes the sense of the verb.

S LV PA   **SLV PA**
The *girl is beautiful.*   *I feel sick.*

Again, this pattern can also be expanded.

The girl I took to the dance *is beautiful* when she smiles.
When I hear about having to go to school this summer, *I feel sick* and want to
    bury my head in the sand.

The portions of the expanded sentences not italicized are modifiers.

Who *is*? "Girl," the subject. What *is* the *girl*? "Beautiful," the predicate adjective.
    tive.
Who *feel*? "I," the subject. *Feel* what? "Sick," the predicate adjective.

PATTERN 3: Subject + Linking Verb + Predicate Noun

This differs from pattern 3 in that the last member is a noun instead
of an adjective.

    S   **LV PN**   **S**   **LV**   **PN**
The policeman is a hero.   My father became a doctor.

Notice that in patterns 3 and 4, the verbs are all verbs of being, seem-
ing, or becoming. They describe a state of being (see 2: PARTS OF
SPEECH: VERBS) and in these two patterns link together, respec-
tively, the subject and predicate adjective and the subject and predicate noun.

PATTERN 4: Subject + Transitive Verb + Direct Object

A *transitive verb* is one that acts *on* something: the *direct object*, the
noun that *receives* the action of the verb.

S TV   **DO**   **S**   **TV**   **DO**
Joe threw the football.   My mother was frying eggs.

S   **TV**   **DO**
Pamela loved Cincinnati.

Who *threw*? "Joe," the subject. *Joe threw* what? "Football," the direct object.
    Do the same for the other two examples.

PATTERN 5: Subject + Transitive Verb + Indirect Object + Direct Object

An *indirect object* is the part of the sentence denoting to whom or for whom an action was performed.

S TV   DO   IO   S   TV   DO   IO
Joe threw the football to Tom.   My mother was frying eggs for my dad.

S TV   IO   DO
I gave my brother some money.

Joe threw what? "Football," the direct object. *Threw the football* to whom? To "Tom," the indirect object. Do the same for the other two examples.

This pattern is frequently found when the verbs indicate action like *giving, lending, sending, mailing, teaching, throwing,* and the like.

PATTERN 6: Subject + Transitive Verb + Direct Object + Object Complement (noun)

The *object complement* acts to further describe or limit the direct object.

S VT   DO   OC
We named our boat *Spraylady*.

Spraylady, the object complement, further describes the *boat* after the action of the verb has been completed.

S VT   DO   OC
The team elected James captain.

Notice that an object complement differs from an adjective in that it cannot be placed *before* the direct object and still make the same sense.

PATTERN 7: Subject + Transitive Verb + Direct Object + Object Complement (adjective)

The only difference between this pattern and pattern 6 is that the object complement is here an adjective.

S TV   DO   OC
They considered the mailman polite.

S TV   DO OC
The snow made my hair wet.

28

As in pattern 6, the object complement cannot be moved to a position that would be appropriate for an ordinary adjective, that is, in front of the direct object.

Notice that

S   TV   DO OC
We painted the fence white

is different in meaning from

S   TV   ADJ DO
We painted the white fence.

---

7 Exercise/PRACTICE WITH THE GRAMMAR OF THE BASIC SENTENCE PATTERNS

A. For each independent clause in each of the sentences below, write in above the main parts the following abbreviations:

S (subject)	IO (indirect object)
VI (intransitive verb)	DO (direct object)
VT (transitive verb)	OCN (object complement, noun)
AUX (auxiliary)	OCAdj (object complement, adjective)
LV (linking verb)	PA (predicate adjective)
	PN (predicate noun)

1. The sky is gray.

2. The fire burned.

3. After awhile, the car stopped.

4. In the morning, Andy makes eggs for breakfast.

5. We elected James chairman.

6. After knowing him two weeks, we thought Paul delightful.

7. Although she was poor, Maggie gave her mother Belgian lace for Christmas.

8. She was religious because she had been raised by religious parents.

9. We were eating lunch when the phone rang.

10. My Aunt Barbara was a member of the Daughters of the American Revolution.

11. As an Easter gift, we mailed my little cousin a basket of colored eggs.

12. She became depressed when she heard the news, but later she seemed lively again.

13. They painted the fence white, but they didn't touch the gate.

14. Professor Miller taught me English grammar and he did it with a sense of humor.

15. Earlier in her career, she had been a policewoman.

    B. Now try to do the same for each dependent clause you find in the sentences you've just worked on.

    C. Write out the sentence patterns called for below. (You may add modifiers wherever you wish.) Label each of the parts.

  1. Pattern 1

_____

_____

  2. Pattern 2

_____

_____

  3. Pattern 3

_____

_____

  4. Pattern 4

_____

_____

  5. Pattern 5

_____

_____

  6. Pattern 6

_____

_____

8 Clauses

Dependent Clauses

A sentence is also called an *independent clause.* It contains a subject and a predicate (which contains at least one finite verb). It is useful to understand that many sentences also contain *dependent*, or *subordinate*, *clauses*, structures that contain a subject and a predicate (which contains at least one finite verb). These are dependent because they cannot stand alone; they must be linked to an independent clause.

I am going to the movies. (Independent clause or sentence.)

SC S V
When I am going to the movies (Dependent, adverbial clause.)

When I am going to the movies, I take along my eyeglasses. (Dependent clause linked to an independent clause.)

Some begin with a relative pronoun which acts as the subject of the clause.

My friend, *who was the ticket taker at the concert*, let me in free. (Dependent clause, beginning with the relative pronoun *who*, which is the subject of the dependent clause.)

Yesterday, I bought a suit *which can be worn either in winter or in summer*. (Dependent clause beginning with the relative pronoun *which*, which is the subject of the dependent clause.)

My girl friend has a sports car *which I use all the time*. (Dependent clause beginning with the relative pronoun *which*, but this time the relative pronoun is *not* the subject; the subject of the clause is *I*.)

The person on campus *who knows me best* is my English professor. (Dependent clause beginning with the relative pronoun *who*, which is also the subject of the clause.)

The person on campus *who I like best* is my English professor. (Dependent clause beginning with *who*; this time the subject is *I*.)

Dependent clauses serve the following functions.

1. *Noun clauses* occupy the same positions in sentences as do single-word nouns or pronouns. They begin with such words as *that*, *who*, *which*, *what*, *whom*, and the like. A noun clause can appear in the sentence in any position usually occupied by a one-word noun.

What I need now is money. (Noun clause with a subject *I* and a verb *need* is the subject of the sentence.)

Money is *what I need now*. (Same clause acts as predicate noun.)

My low bank balance shows *what I need now*. (Same clause as direct object of verb *shows*.)

2. *Adjective clauses* modify nouns, pronouns, or strings of words that act like nouns just as single-word adjectives do. They begin with relative pronouns (*that, which, who, whom, what*) or other clause markers like *whose, whatever, where, why,* and *how.*

The car *that I bought last year* is falling apart. (Modifies the noun *car.*)

She took me to the best French restaurant *that she knew.* (Modifies the noun *restaurant.*)

3. *Adverb clauses* modify verbs, adjectives, other adverbs, or even whole sentences.

When you're in a hurry, you make mistakes. (Modifies *make*, the verb of the main clause.)

You look as good *as you can.* (Modifies the adjective *good.*)

An important point to notice about some adverb clauses—particularly those that begin with subordinating conjunctions—is that, unlike adjective clauses, they can be repositioned in the sentence without changing its meaning.

When you're in a hurry, you make mistakes.

You make mistakes *when you're in a hurry.*

Sentences Containing Elliptical Clauses

Frequently a clause is written with one or more words omitted. The expression is still a clause but we call it an elliptical one.

When driving, I always fasten my seat belt. (Omitted from the italicized clause are the words *I am*, which are understood.)

On the picnic, Lisa brought the food and *Donna the drinks.* (Missing from the italicized clause is the word *brought.*)

Note: When dependent clauses are punctuated as if they are sentences, they are called sentence fragments.

8 Exercise/IDENTIFYING AND CONSTRUCTING DEPENDENT CLAUSES

A. In the blank space after each italicized clause, identify it as either dependent or independent; if it is dependent, identify it with the letters ADV (adverb), ADJ (adjective), or NOUN to describe its function in the sentence.

> *Example*   The men *who are working in the road* ____ADJ____ have been at it all morning.

1. *Although he remembered to buy the butter,* _____ he forgot to bring home the bacon.

2. My little boy ate the apples *which I had planned to use in the pie.* _____

3. Many Americans are pessimistic about the future these days; *nevertheless, a few of us still believe the future is rosy.* _____

4. *Unless I'm mistaken,* _____ you and I met at a party last month, *although I can't remember your name.* _____

5. Some people let their pets do *whatever they* please. _____

6. *That the painting is beautiful* _____ is obvious if you look at it closely enough.

7. *Whatever Joe offers to pay me for damaging my car* _____ will be satisfactory, *unless it's really an unreasonable sum.* _____

8. For Christmas, I got a camera, *which I traded in for a calculator,* _____ and a new TV set *that I returned for cash.* _____

9. *Although he had just begun to practice,* _____ Bob was the attorney *whom the court appointed to defend Johnson.* _____

10. *What needs fixing* _____ should be sent to the repair shop; *frankly, I can't repair things* _____ *because I'm a mechanical idiot.* _____

B. Below you are given a set of basic sentence patterns. Construct clauses to add to each according to the specifications given.

Example   Cats are animals. (Add an adjective clause.)
              Cats are animals that can scratch.

1. Emily is beautiful. (Add an adverb clause.)

_____

_____

2. My father remarried. (Add an adjective clause.)

_____

_____

3. Jackson hits homers. (Add an adjective clause.)

_____

_____

4. We considered our mother a saint. (Add an adverb clause.)

_____

_____

5. This tractor eats gas. (Add an adjective clause.)

_____

_____

9 Phrases

A phrase is a group of related words that has neither a subject nor a verb. Phrases may appear in sentences as subjects, direct or indirect objects, objects of a preposition, object complements, predicate adjectives, or predicate nouns. They can also be used as modifiers. Phrases are classified by the kinds of words with which they begin, their headwords.

Verbal Phrases

1. An *infinitive phrase* begins with an infinitive, the form of the verb containing the word *to*, for example, *to love, to kiss, to play*. Infinitive phrases may also contain modifiers or the object of the infinitive or both.

Infinitive phrase as subject:

To play basketball well is difficult. (*Basketball* is the object of the infinitive, *well* its modifier.)

Infinitive phrase as direct object:

I love *to spend money.* (*Money* is the object of *to spend,* the whole phrase the object of *love.*)

Infinitive phrase as modifier:

I work *to make money.* (Again, *money* is the object, this time of the infinitive *to make.* The whole phrase modifies *work* and is thus an adverb phrase.)

Infinitive phrase as predicate noun:

The point of the game is *to score goals.*

Infinitive phrase as an object complement:

Uncle Arthur has money *to throw away.*

2. A *participial phrase* begins with either a present participle (the *-ing* form of the verb) or a past participle and includes modifiers or complements or both. Participial phrases function in the sentence as adjectives.

Sleeping soundly, James did not notice the gifts we placed under his crib. (*Soundly* modifies the participle; the whole phrase modifies *James*.)

Known for his musical ability, William had never had any formal instruction. (*Known* is the past particple; *for his musical ability* is a phrase modifying *known*, but the whole italicized portion of the sentence modifies *William*.)

3. A *gerund phrase* begins with a *gerund* (an *-ing* verb used as a noun) and includes its modifiers or objects or both. Gerund phrases always function as nouns.

Riding a bicycle is fun. (*Bicycle* is the object of *riding*, the gerund, and the whole phrase is a noun, the subject of the sentence.)

I love *talking to my wife*. (The whole phrase is the object of the verb *love*; *to my wife* is the object of the gerund *talking*.)

Prepositional Phrases

A *prepositional phrase* begins with a preposition and always includes the object of the preposition (a noun); however, it can also include a determiner (e.g., *a, the, an, his, my*) and a modifier or both. A prepositional phrase can function in the sentence as an adverb, an adjective, or sometimes as a noun.

The man *in the blue suit* looks like a lawyer. (*In* = preposition; *suit* = object of the preposition; *the* = determiner; *blue* = modifies *suit*; the whole phrase is an adjective modifying *man*.)

The president arrived *at the airport*. (The whole phrase modifies *arrived* and is an adverb; *at* = preposition; *the* = determiner; *airport* = object of *at*.)

Over the fence is a home run. (The whole phrase is a noun, the subject of the sentence; *over* = preposition; *fence* = object of the preposition; *the* = determiner.)

---

9 Exercise/IDENTIFICATION AND CONSTRUCTION OF PHRASES

A. For each italicized phrase in the sentences below, write in the blank space provided the kind of phrase it is and its function in the sentence.

Example   I went *to the supermarket* yesterday.

prepositional phrase; adverb; modifies went.

1. He lived *in his father's house* for a year.

2. *Taking a stand against crime*, John volunteered for his local street patrol.

36

3. I loved *taking her hand in mine.*

_____

4. Considering what's known about the importance of fitness, *to be out of shape* is foolish.

_____

5. *Flying very low,* the pilot suddenly gunned the engine.

_____

6. *Defeated by the rain,* we gave up our baseball game and went to the movies.

_____

7. The people *in the neighborhood* thought I was crazy, but I loved my purple house.

_____

8. It's awful *to be in love* and not be loved in return.

_____

9. *Traveling by boat* seems luxurious these days.

_____

10. *After dinner* will be too late.

_____

11. He handed his ticket to a man *standing at the gate.*

_____

12. I hated *living in a tent.*

_____

13. We were happy *to begin our vacation.*

_____

14. My aunt is *from California.*

_____

15. It's time *to be reasonable.*

_____

    B. Construct sentences containing phrases written to the following specifications.

      Example   (a prepositional phrase used as an adjective)

              The man *in the easy* chair is my uncle.

  1. (a prepositional phrase used as an adverb)

_____

  2. (a participial phrase, using the past participle: adjective)

_____

  3. (an infinitive phrase used as an adverb)

_____

  4. (an infinitive phrase used as an adjective)

_____

  5. (a gerund phrase used as an object)

_____

  6. (a prepositional phrase used as an adverb)

_____

  7. (a participial phrase—present participle—used as an adjective)

_____

  8. (a gerund phrase used as a subject)

_____

9. (a prepositional phrase used as a noun)

_____

10. (a participial phrase, using a past participle)

_____

10 Appositives

An *appositive*, a word or phrase or some structure that can take the place of a noun, is set beside a noun or pronoun or noun subject to further explain or define it by actually renaming it. In the following examples, the first noun is in italics and the appositive in boldface.

The *detective*, **Reilly**, spoke very slowly. (Appositive word.)
Isiah Thomas's *skill*, **stuffing a basketball through a hoop**, earns him a large salary. (Phrase as appositive.)
For Christmas, I got a *camera*, **a Kodak Instamatic**.

An appositive that is essential to identify its noun is not separated from it by commas. Such an appositive is called *restrictive*.

My brother *Mac* lives in New York. (*Mac* is essential in identifying *brother*—since I have other brothers.)
The gas station attendant *John* gave my car a lube job. (Again, *John* is essential—to distinguish him from other attendants.)

However, some appositives are nonrestrictive—they are *not* essential to identify the noun—and therefore require commas:

The state capital, *Albany*, lies on the Hudson River.
George, *a friend for many years*, is coming to dinner tonight.
For Christmas, I got a *camera*, *a Kodak Instamatic*.

(See also 49 Internal Punctuation II, page 245, for more on *restrictive* and *nonrestrictive*.)

10 Exercise/IDENTIFYING AND CONSTRUCTING APPOSITIVES

A. Underline and correctly punctuate (where necessary) all the appositives in the sentences below.

1. George the only musician in the group sat down at the piano.

2. In the woods, she would need only three things a blanket, a fishing line and some matches.

3. My professor Norman Kelvin wrote a book on E. M. Forster.

4. I have an appointment tonight with Professor Quinn, the senior English adviser.
5. Everybody climbed into the car an old and battered blue sedan.
6. My aunt Rose Solomon is nearly 100 years old.
7. We were in the hands of the mediator, the one who would settle the argument.
8. Dennis Turner my film professor knows everything there is to know about movies.
9. The police arrested two people, a burglar and a robber.
10. The fighter we were most eager to see Jackson was not on the bill that night.

   B. Write sentences using the appositives called for.

   Example   an old building on North Main Street
                We went to the garage, an old building on North Main Street.

1. (Charley Wells)

   _____

2. (a friend I met at college)

   _____

3. (the only one who ever cared about me)

   _____

4. (a wonderful person, a dear friend, an outstanding citizen)

   _____

5. (a surging, swaying mass)

   _____

11 Exercise/BASIC GRAMMAR REVIEW TEST

A. Name the parts of speech to which the italicized words belong. Use the blanks next to these words to write in the names.

> *Example*   The *garden* ___noun___ *rarely* ___adv.___ looked more
>
> *beautiful* ___adj.___ .

1. We *went* _____ *to* _____ the party wearing *our* _____

   _____ dinner jackets, *which* _____ , of course, we had rented.

2. *Although* _____ we were tired, we danced.

B. Name the basic parts of the following sentences. Above each part print the name according to the list of abbreviations given on page 29. Ignore for now the modifiers, clauses, and phrases.

1. On Christmas Eve, we threw a noisy party for the whole dorm.

2. Charles smoked a great deal, but he wasn't happy about it.

3. Terry seemed sad when she came home last night.

4. To put it plainly, he's a prince!

5. Lugging that heavy suitcase to the post office, I mailed it to my mother in California.

C. In each of the following sentences you will find either a phrase or a dependent clause. Underline each. Then, in the space above each, write its function in the sentence.

> adverb clause
> *Example*   When she arrived, she was carrying her suitcase.

1. The lake in Davenport has very deep water.

2. People who cannot think for themselves usually speak in clichés.

3. Having a few extra dollars that week, I bought myself a new shirt.

4. To draw water from the well was a hard job.

5. Without anybody's assistance, I learned woodworking and built my own furniture.

6. The man in the blue suit is my date for tonight.

7. The thing that hurts most about failing that math exam is that I studied for it for weeks.

8. Because he loved me so much, he gave me the ring that his mother had given him for his last birthday.

9. He wanted to study medicine, but he couldn't afford the cost.

10. Someone I knew in high school is transferring to this college.

   D. Give a name to each italicized part in the following sentences. Beside the name, write the function of that part in the sentence.

1. We elected George *chairman* of the committee.

2. *Through the night,* she drove *steadily.*

3. The *athlete who comes here on a scholarship* has to keep up his grade point average.

4. *Riding a motorcycle* can be dangerous *to your health.*

5. *Watching carefully,* I could see the *fish darting along the bottom.*

Sentence Faults

12 Sentence Fragments

Only an independent clause may be punctuated as a sentence, that is, with a capital letter at the beginning and a period at the end. Whenever we find a dependent clause, any kind of phrase, or certain other structures punctuated as if they were sentences, we call them *sentence fragments*. Ordinarily, these fragments belong with an adjacent sentence, either the one preceding or the one following the fragment; but it is possible to correct them in other ways than merely joining them to the nearest independent clause. Sometimes these other ways are more effective.

1. Correcting fragments made of *dependent clauses:*

Fragment Until we went to the movies.
Revised We went to the movies. (Method 1: We have removed the subordinating conjunction. Now the structure is independent, a sentence.)
Revised Until we went to the movies, *we were doing homework.* (Method 2: We have added an independent clause. Note that in this case, an adverb clause, we could have added the independent clause at either end.)
Fragment He took a course in world literature. *Which was being offered by the French Department.*
Revised He took a course in world literature, which was being offered by the French Department. (Method 3: The clause is simply linked to the independent clause preceding it and to which it belongs; it modifies the words *world literature.*)

2. Correcting fragments made of *-ing* phrases:

Fragment Swimming in the ocean.
Revised *I was* swimming in the ocean. (The participle, *swimming*, has been made into a complete verb by the addition of *was*, and the subject *I* has been added. The structure is now an independent clause, a sentence.)
Revised Swimming in the ocean, *I saw a sailboat.* (The phrase has been attached to an independent clause.)

3. Correcting fragments made of *infinitive phrases* and *prepositional phrases:*

Fragment He had every intention of leaving town. *To start a new life in the West.*
Revised He had every intention of leaving town to start a new life in the West.
Fragment She wanted to celebrate graduation. *With her whole sorority, her family, and her friends.*

Revised She wanted to celebrate graduation with her whole sorority, her family, and her friends.

4. Correcting fragments made of other structures:

Fragment His name was Robert. *A charmer, a con man, a swindler.* (This is a final appositive and must be linked to the independent clause with either a comma or a dash.)

Revised His name was Robert, a charmer, a con man, a swindler.

Fragment She was given one scholarship by her mother's union. *And another by the university.* (The fragment is one part of the compound object of the verb *given*.)

Revised She was given one scholarship by her mother's union and another by the university.

---

12 Exercise/IDENTIFYING AND CORRECTING SENTENCE FRAGMENTS

A. Which of the structures printed below are dependent (either dependent clauses or any of the various kinds of phrases) and which independent? Write your answers in the spaces provided.

1. Swimming in the ocean. _____

2. With all my heart. _____

3. I jog every day. _____

4. After we woke up. _____

5. When we told them. _____

6. To watch television. _____

7. Fish swim. _____

8. To play basketball. _____

9. Having a headache. _____

10. Which he wanted. _____

11. In a few years. _____

12. After we had gone a mile, we stopped. _____

13. In a few years. _____

14. Although it was late, we continued to talk. _____

15. Because she laughed. _____

B. Below are printed sentence fragments made of the structures we have been discussing in this section. Identify the type of structure each is made of and then correct it.

48

1. She said she was determined to spend four years at college. Although she would find it difficult to pay the costs.

_____

_____

2. Swimming all by myself in the great expanse of ocean. I was really scared out of my wits.

_____

_____

3. After a good lunch, we went down to inspect the barn. Which looked to us as if it had been built in the middle of the last century.

_____

_____

4. She had only one thing in mind for her career. To spend her most productive years working in the service of the poor and oppressed.

_____

_____

5. While visiting his old campus, Noah decided to drop in and see Professor Keating. An old friend, an excellent adviser, an uncommonly fine teacher and scholar.

_____

_____

6. No matter how hard he tried, he just couldn't manage to start the car. Which he had a good mind to get rid of because it was giving him so much trouble.

_____

_____

7. There are three things absolutely necessary to achieve success in this world. A first-class education, the right kind of attitude toward other people, and a fanatical dedication to hard work.

8. Once he had made up his mind to take a walk, he started to walk confidently and even with pleasure. Toward the lake in the middle of the woods that was ringed with slender pine trees.

_____

_____

_____

9. Sally and Joe had just returned home to Brooklyn. From their trip to Paris, Rome, and London.

_____

_____

_____

10. All at once, through a hole in the clouds, we saw the plane. Flying very low over the rooftops, making little dips toward the ground, as if it were going to crash.

_____

_____

_____

11. Everybody hopes for peace in the vast area we call the Middle East. A place nobody in the West knows very much about.

_____

_____

_____

12. For Christmas, Maggie bought Alan a new Pentax camera. Which didn't please him very much but which he considered valuable anyway.

_____

_____

_____

13. She wrote him that he needn't call or write her. Unless he was ready to discuss their relationship seriously.

_____

_____

_____

14. It was necessary for him to be on campus no later than Friday, the twenty-seventh. Because after that date he would have to pay a late registration fee.

_____

_____

_____

15. After much haggling, the Admissions Committee agreed to a meeting with me on Saturday. To discuss my application and my financial situation.

_____

_____

_____

C. The following passage contains a number of sentence fragments. Rewrite it in the space provided, correcting all the fragments you can find.

Most Americans nowadays are worried. About inflation and the high cost of living. They are really feeling more and more frustrated. Because they are finding it harder and harder to make ends meet. Although some families have tried to solve the problem by pooling several incomes. People still find rising prices hard to cope with. Nobody is really certain. Of what's ahead tomorrow or the next day. Therefore, people resort to all kinds of tricks. To stay ahead of the game and feed their families. For example, many people have formed food co-ops. To lower the cost of those necessities. Some people band together to rent summer campsites. For cheaper vacations for everybody. Some skip vacations entirely. Although wage earners need the recreation. Some people have even begun to trade on the "black market." A kind of network where second-hand goods and services are bartered. Financial worries that motivate people to behave in such ways are likely to determine the course of politics in this country. Unless the politicians do something about it quickly.

_____

_____

_____

_____

_____

_____

_____

_____

_____

_____

_____

13 The Comma Splice and the Run-On Sentence

Comma splice is the name we give to two independent clauses (or sentences) when they are joined (or *spliced* together) *only* by a comma.

The police found the victim lying in a pool of blood, he had been shot once in the left temple.

If the comma were missing entirely, we should call the error a *fused* or *run-on sentence.* Neither comma splices nor run-on sentences are punctuated correctly, but either one may be corrected in one of four ways: (1) The two independent clauses can be joined by a comma followed by one of the coordinating conjunctions; (2) they can be separated by a period; (3) they can be separated by a semicolon; (4) they can be linked by a comma if one of the clauses is first made subordinate (or dependent).

Comma Splice The police found the victim lying in a pool of blood, he had been shot once in the left temple.

Revised by Method 1 The police found the victim lying in a pool of blood, *for* he had been shot once in the left temple.

Revised by Method 2 The police found the victim lying in a pool of blood. *He* had been shot once in the left temple.

Revised by Method 3 The police found the victim lying in a pool of blood; he had been shot once in the left temple.

Revised by Method 4 *When* the police found the victim lying in a pool of blood, he had been shot once in the left temple.

---

13 Exercise/RECOGNIZING INDEPENDENT CLAUSES; CORRECTING THE COMMA SPLICE AND THE RUN-ON SENTENCE

A. Each group of words given below contains at least two independent clauses, although some contain more than two. Place brackets around each.

1. Ellen had her hands full taking care of Stephen, he was at the age where he was full of mischief.

2. The sky turned gray bolts of lightning flashed in the east thunder rolled across the mountains.

3. Americans are more conscious of the need for fitness, they have become active sports enthusiasts, they are more interested in good nutrition, they are aware of the need to reduce stress.

4. Television can be entertaining, it can also be boring.

5. Children learn from their parent's examples parents' behavior is an important part of their experience.

6. The life of a farmer is a lonely one his opportunities to socialize are limited because of the constant attention he must give to the things he cultivates.

7. Oil imports are very expensive, we must learn to be economical in our use of energy, this may require us to adapt to a new way of living.

8. Communications makes the world smaller, people are thus brought closer together, we find ourselves with common interests.

9. Some scientists call the computer essentially "stupid" others fear its capacity to "think."

10. College freshmen need help making the transition from high school, the sheer size of most colleges can be a problem to new students.

B. Below are pairs of sentences. Some are correctly punctuated and some not. First, identify the sentences that are correctly punctuated; then try linking each pair, correct or not, with a comma followed by one of the coordinating conjunctions: *and, but, or, nor, for, yet, so.*

1. He decided to buy a new car. The old one was a wreck.

   _____

   _____

2. He liked her, something about her bothered him.

   _____

   _____

3. He could spend the whole weekend studying. He could take Sunday off and go to the beach.

   _____

   _____

4. She knew what she wanted. She was determined to get it.

_____

_____

5. The last bus had gone he decided to walk.

_____

_____

6. Big cars are beautiful and luxurious, they eat too much gas.

_____

_____

7. Television movies are interrupted by too many commercials the commercials pay for the entertainment.

_____

_____

8. My beach vacation started on July 1. By the third, I was as red as a lobster.

_____

_____

9. Working part-time is profitable for students, it prepares them for the working world.

_____

_____

10. Nina could speak French, of course. She knew no English.

_____

_____

C. Some of the pairs of sentences below are run-ons or comma splices. These should be linked by a semicolon. After you have supplied the semicolon, look at the list of conjunctive adverbs which follows and see if the addition of one of these might create a better relation between the two sentences: *anyway, besides, consequently, finally, furthermore, however, instead, meanwhile, moreover, nevertheless, otherwise, subsequently, therefore, thus.* Next to the pairs that are correctly punctuated mark a *C* (for *correct*).

1. My uncle wears an orange tie with his green suit, he must be color-blind.

_____

_____

2. Fred isn't going to summer school this year he's going backpacking in the Sierras.

_____

_____

3. I have to study this afternoon and can't play basketball, my legs hurt.

_____

_____

4. Buying a car is cheap; operating it is expensive.

_____

_____

5. She didn't look good in jeans, they were too informal.

_____

_____

6. The two-party system of American politics is pretty chaotic, it works most of the time.

_____

_____

7. We will have to find alternate sources of energy our economy will suffer from excessive oil imports.

_____

_____

8. Financial aid for students should be increased; tuition costs are just too high for most American families.

_____

_____

9. He washed the dishes, put the cat out, set the alarm clock, he brushed his teeth and went to bed.

_____

_____

10. In the early 1980s, he worked as a paralegal secretary, he went to law school and passed the bar.

_____

_____

D. Below are pairs of independent clauses incorrectly linked by a comma only. Make each pair grammatically correct by subordinating one member of the pair through the addition of a subordinating conjunction. (Some subordinating conjunctions: *when, as, if, because, although, whenever, while, after, unless, until.*)

1. He did the dishes, he took a walk.

_____

2. The movie was popular, there was a long line to get in.

_____

3. She was convinced Tom was sincere, she went out with him.

_____

4. The weather was cool, he wore only a T-shirt.

   _____

5. Ellen was saving her money she wanted to buy a fur coat.

   _____

6. She was only an art student, she could draw with great skill.

   _____

7. He decided to go the beach it rained.

   _____

8. He could take Susan out for a big dinner, he had enough money.

   _____

9. He couldn't borrow money from Ed, he was angry at him.

   _____

10. Pittsburgh made a habit of losing the Super Bowl, they had some very good players.

   _____

   E. Rewrite each of the following sentence pairs in four ways to correct either the comma splice or the run-on sentence. (1) Use a coordinating conjunction and a comma; (2) make two sentences by using a period between the members; (3) use a semicolon with or without a conjunctive adverb; (4) make one member of the pair a dependent clause through the use of a subordinating conjunction.

   Example   He liked to swim, he went to the beach often.

(coord. conj. + comma)	He liked to swim, and he went to the beach often.
(semicolon)	He liked to swim; he went to the beach often.
	He liked to swim; therefore, he went to the beach often.
(two sentences)	He liked to swim. He went to the beach often.
(dep. clause + sub. conj.)	Because he liked to swim, he went to the beach often.

1. We had met several times I didn't know him very well.

   (coord. conj. + comma)

   _____

   (two sentences)

   _____

   (semicolon)

   _____

   (dep. clause + sub. conj.)

   _____

2. She studies very hard, her grades are high.

   (coord. conj. + comma)

   _____

   (two sentences)

   _____

   (semicolon)

   _____

   (dep. clause + sub. conj.)

   _____

3. Most television programming is boring. I don't own a set.

   (coord. conj. + comma)

   _____

   (two sentences)

   _____

59

(semicolon)

_____

(sub. conj. + dep. clause)

_____

4. He couldn't stand the taste of meat, he became a vegetarian.

(coord. conj. + comma)

_____

(two sentences)

_____

(semicolon)

_____

(sub. conj. + dep. clause)

_____

5. Linda has talent it will take her a long way.

(coord. conj. + comma)

_____

(two sentences)

_____

(semicolon)

_____

(sub. conj. + dep. clause)

_____

6. The days are getting shorter, winter is coming.

(coord. conj. + comma)

_____

(two sentences)

_____

(semicolon)

_____

(sub. conj. + dep. clause)

_____

7. Joanna is very beautiful, she looks like a model.

(coord. conj. + comma)

_____

(two sentences)

_____

(semicolon)

_____

(sub. conj. + dep. clause)

_____

14 Case

Nouns in English have two cases: the common form, *doctor*, for example, which is used when that word is a subject, object, and so forth; and the possessive form or case, *doctor's*, which denotes possession.

Problems with case arise with pronouns, which have three cases: *nominative*, *possessive*, and *objective*.

	Personal Pronouns			Relative Pronouns		
	Nom.	Poss.	Obj.	Nom.	Poss.	Obj.
	Singular			*Singular*		
1st Person	I	my, mine	me	who	whose	whom
2nd Person	you*	your, yours	you			
3d Person	he, she, it*	his, her, hers, its	him			
			her			
			it			
	Plural			*Plural*		
1st Person	we	our, ours	us, it	who	whose	whom
2nd Person	you	your, yours	you			
3d Person	they	their, theirs	them			

*As you can see, *it* and *you* do not change in the objective case, only in the possessive.

Use the Nominative Case

1. When the word is the subject:

We [not *us*] want to go to the movies.

2. When *who* is the subject of the verb in a clause:

Lisa is the one *who* we think is most gullible. (*Who* is the subject of *is*.)

3. In formal writing after forms of the verb *be* (*is, are, was, were*, and so forth):

Formal   It is *I*. It might be *they*.
Informal   It's *me*. It might be *them*.

4. In formal writing, after the conjunctions *as* and *than*.

Formal   He is healthier than *I* [am]. We are as intelligent as *they* [are].
Informal   He is healthier than *me*. We are as intelligent as *them*.

5. When the pronoun appears as part of a compound subject:

Jason and *he* [or *He* and Jason] played basketball yesterday. (Subjects: Jason, *he*.)

6. In an appositive, which further identifies or explains the noun/subject:

Those two—Dennis and *he*—have known each other for years.

Use the Possessive Case

1. To indicate possession, source, authorship, and similar relationships:

I liked *his* house.
I know *whose* dog that is.
The show has *its* good moments.

2. In formal writing, before a *gerund* (the *-ing* form of a verb that is used as a noun):

Formal   She was happy about *his trading* in the car.
Informal   She was happy about *him trading* in the car.

Use the Objective Case

1. Where the pronoun is the object of a verb, whether the object is simple or compound:

Simple   The idea amused *him* [or *me*].
Compound   The committee appointed *Paul and me* to make the arrangements.

Note: In certain questions, the first word is the object:

Whom did you ask? (*Whom* is the object of *did ask*.)

2. When the pronoun is the object of a verbal (the *-ing* or the infinitive form of the verb):

Kiss*ing him* was a pleasure.
To know him was *to love him*.

3. When the pronoun is the object of a preposition:

None *of them* knew my name.
Buckley is the professor *for whom* I have the greatest respect.

Note: When two pronouns are objects of the same preposition, both must be in the objective case:

You will have to choose *between him* and *me*.

4. In formal writing, where *whom* is clearly the object of the verb in a clause:

Formal   Jacqueline was the aunt *whom* we loved best. (*Whom* is the object of *loved*.)
Informal   Jacqueline was the aunt *who* we loved best.

Note: Even though *whom* is falling into disuse, good formal writing demands that it always be used after a preposition:

Of *whom* are you speaking?
He didn't know to *whom* it should be sent.

5. Of a pronoun when following the conjunctions *as* and *than* if that pronoun is the object of an omitted verb:

He gives her more than [he gives] *me*. (*Me* is the object of *gives*.)
I loved her as much as [I loved] *him*. (*Him* is the object of *loved*.)

---

14   Exercise/SELECTING THE CORRECT CASE OF THE PRONOUN

A. Use each of the following pronouns correctly in a sentence.

1. who (where it is the subject of a verb in a clause)

_____

_____

2. whom (following a preposition)

_____

_____

3. us

_____

_____

4. them

_____

_____

64

5. the proper form of the male personal pronoun before an -*ing* gerund

_____

_____

B. Two pronouns are shown in parentheses in each of the following sentences. Cross out the one that is incorrect, following formal usage.

Example   There is absolute trust between Arthur and (me, ~~I~~).

1. They elected Ed and (me, I) cochairmen.
2. Maggie is as energetic as (me, I).
3. When Linsey answered the doorbell, she knew it was (he, him).
4. Arthur and (him, he) were very rich men.
5. The two of us, David and (I, me) published books that year.
6. We couldn't locate any of the professors (who, whom) we thought were our advisors.
7. IBM gave the jobs to two applicants, Ingrid and (me, I).
8. (Who, Whom) were you asking for?
9. I love my little brother, but I can live without (his, him) following me around every minute.
10. She was certainly older than (me, I).
11. The president, (he, him) alone, is responsible for foreign policy.
12. I can't imagine (him, his) running more than a mile.
13. Brody was the professor to (who, whom) I owed the most.
14. The new man they hired simply isn't as good as (I, me).
15. Richard and (she, her) dined together every night.
16. She couldn't get used to (his, him) practicing the piano for hours on end.
17. The woman to (who, whom) you are referring is my wife!
18. The Yankees are every bit as good a team as (they, them).
19. She was angry about (their, them) raising their voices.
20. He conceded defeat when he realized he didn't have as many votes as (she, her).

15 Subject-Verb Agreement, Part 1

A singular subject requires a singular verb and a plural subject a plural verb. Trouble with these requirements is found in the present tense, where the ending of the verb in the third person singular is always *-s*.

She *looks* beautiful.
He *seems* drunk.
It *appears* to be a nice day.

Problems also arise where the subject becomes more complicated and you must decide whether the subject is singular or plural.

1. For compound subjects—those joined by the word *and*—use a plural verb:

Harvey and Al *play* tennis together.

2. For subjects separated by *neither . . . nor* or *either . . . or*, the following rules apply: When both subjects are singular, use a singular verb:

Neither my uncle nor my aunt *knows* Spanish.

When one of the subjects is plural, use the verb that agrees with the closest one:

For dessert, either fruits or *ice cream is* all right.
Neither my brother nor his *friends drive* cars.

When a compound subject consists of two items that can be thought of as a single unit, use a singular verb.

---

15 Exercise/WORKING WITH SUBJECT-VERB AGREEMENT

A. Change each of the sentences below, following the procedure of the example.

> *Example*   Fred's *obsession is* books.
> *Change*   *Books are* Fred's obsession.

You can see that the verb must change because the subject has changed in number.

1. His main interest is stamps.

   _____

2. Swimming and golf are my only recreation.

   _____

3. Our greatest need is friends.

   _____

4. Diet and exercise are my only possible course of action.

   _____

5. The Turks are our fiercest enemy.

   _____

6. His diversion is late night television movies.

   _____

7. Busby Berkeley's fantasy is a thousand dancing girls.

   _____

8. The sciences are the missing link in Lisa's education.

   _____

9. Mother's only demand of us is good manners.

   _____

10. The school's greatest strength is the students.

    _____

B. Change each of the sentences given below, following the procedure of the example.

    Example   *She* said *she plays* the piano.
    Change   *They* said *they play* the piano.

67

1. She surprises herself when she finds she has no money at the end of the week.

They _____

2. They hint that they are fed up.

She _____

3. He hopes he wins the lottery.

They _____

4. After spending all night on the train, they wonder if they'll ever reach Paris.

After spending all night on the train, he _____

5. She said she eats too much late at night.

They _____

6. They pray they find an apartment in New York.

She _____

7. He admitted he drinks too much.

They _____

8. They said they play to win.

He _____

9. She estimates she earns $50,000 a year.

They _____

10. She feels she is being misled by the news reports.

They _____

C. In some of the sentences below, the subject and verb agree. Next to these, write *C*. For the others, underline the complete subject and verb and decide whether these are singular or plural. Correct the lack of agreement between subject and verb by changing one or the other.

1. _____ Soup and sandwiches is on the menu every day.

68

2. _____ Is the tip and the sales tax included in the price?
3. _____ Neither Lisa nor Tom think their marriage will be a success.
4. _____ Either the butler or the gardener are responsible for the murder.
5. _____ Meat, milk, fruit, and vegetables are all components of a healthy diet.
6. _____ Peter and John begin their European tour in February.
7. _____ The guitarist and the drummer writes all the songs for the band.
8. _____ Foreign policy and inflation is the main issues of the election campaign.
9. _____ Neither Tony nor his friends plays tennis.
10. _____ Either Carole King or Perry Como is the best-selling recording artist in history.

16 Subject-Verb Agreement, Part 2

The following rules will help you to determine if a particular subject is singular or plural.

1. Collective nouns like *army*, *audience*, *class*, *faculty*, *committee*, *team*, and *public* usually take the singular verb because they are thought of as single units.

The *team is* in first place.
The *crowd cheers* every play.

2. Collective nouns such as *plurality*, *minority*, *mass*, and *majority* may take either singular or plural verbs, depending on how you use them.

A *minority* of students *are* majoring in Sanskrit. (*Minority* is plural because it stands here for separate students.)
A *minority* of the population *votes* the straight Democratic ticket. (*Minority* here stands for a single political unity—the unit that votes the straight Democratic ticket.)

3. Where a subject is modified either by a phrase or a clause, consider only the number of the simple subject. The verb must agree with that subject alone, not with a word or words in the modifier.

Subject Modified by a Phrase
Jogging by oneself or with friends *is* healthful exercise.
simple subject
full subject

Subject Modified by a Clause
A *child* who makes mistakes *earns* the sympathy of his parents.
simple subject
full subject

16 Exercise/CHOOSING THE CORRECT VERB FOR SUBJECTS MODIFIED BY CLAUSES AND PHRASES

Underline the simple subject of each of the following sentences. Then, ignoring the phrase or clause that modifies it, read the sentence to determine which of the verbs in parentheses agrees with that subject. Cross out the incorrect verb.

> *Example* People living in this apartment house (~~is~~, are) not likely to know their neighbors.

1. The songs that Bill sings to James (is, are) hilarious.
2. The change of the seasons in northern Vermont (is, are) dramatic.
3. The difference between men and women (is, are) that women are more introspective.
4. A professor who speaks in monotones (become, becomes) boring after awhile.
5. Children who eat a lot of sweets or sugar (develop, develops) cavities.
6. Donna's need for attention from her friends and family (belie, belies) her desire to be loved.
7. The violence depicted in some television programs and movies (influence, influences) young viewers adversely.
8. A miracle drug that can cure all diseases (sound, sounds) suspicious.
9. The smell of freshly ironed clothes (remind, reminds) me of my grandmother.
10. The optical illusions in the drawings of M. C. Escher (confound, confounds) the viewer.

17 Subject-Verb Agreement: Special Kinds of Subjects, Part 3

The following rules apply to special kinds of subjects you will ordinarily find in your writing.

1. The following pronouns are singular and take singular verbs:

anybody	each	everyone	nobody
anything	either	everything	none
anyone	everybody	neither	no one
somebody	someone	something	one

Everything you say *is* relevant.
Each works long hours.
Everyone knows his own mind.

2. Words ending in *-ics*—such as *mathematics, economics, politics,* and *dialectics*—are singular and take singular verbs when you are speaking of the subject as a whole—as *one* thing.

Mathematics is a subject that never gave me trouble.
Economics does not have all the answers the business world needs.

Where these terms refer to a number or collection of separate ideas rather than a singular entity, they take a plural verb.

My uncle's *politics do* not *agree* with mine. (The series of ideas that constitute his *politics*.)
Radical *economics see* the spectre of inflation everywhere. (A number of separate economic ideas.)

3. Where you use the phrase *one of those which* or *one of those who,* the first verb you use must be plural, the second singular.

One of those people *who insist* on promptness *is* my history professor. (The first verb, *insist,* is plural, agreeing with the word after *those—people—*and the second verb, *is,* is singular, agreeing with the first word of the sentence, *one.*)

4. In the case of the phrases *there is* and *there are,* the verb choice does not depend on *there—*which is not the subject of sentences beginning with these phrases. Rather it depends on what follows the verb—which is the subject of the sentence.

There *are eggs* in the refrigerator. (*Eggs*, the plural subject, requires the plural *are*.)

There *is* a *ghost* in the house. (*Ghost*, the singular subject, takes the singular *is*.)

5. The phrase *the number of* always takes a singular verb; the phrase *a number of* always takes a plural verb.

A number of my pots *are* hanging on the wall.
The number of pots hanging on the wall *is* sufficient.

(In both cases, *number* is the subject; in the first case, however, *number* refers to quantity seen as several units—thus plural; in the second, the word refers to a quantity seen as a unit—thus singular.)

6. The words *part* and *portion* always take the singular verb because they always signify a single unit or fraction.

Part of my apartment *has* nothing in it but plants.
A *portion* of ices *is* a satisfactory dessert.

7. A parenthetical expression introduced by phrases such as *together with*, *as well as*, *in addition to*, and *including* does not affect the agreement of the subject and the verb.

The fire engine *and* the police car *are* racing toward the fire. (Compound subject joined by *and* requires a plural verb.)
The fire engine, *as well as* the police car, *is* racing toward the fire. (The singular subject is now *fire engine*; *police car* is now part of the parenthetical expression introduced by *as well as* and does not count in determining the subject.)

---

17 Exercise/AGREEMENT OF VERBS WITH SPECIAL KINDS OF SUBJECTS

In each of the sentences below, cross out the verb in parentheses that does not agree with the italicized subject.

1. *One* of these people (is, are) lying.
2. *Politics* (is, are) not a suitable subject for innocent people to study.
3. *Economics 156* (involve, involves) the theory of supply and demand.
4. *Olivia*, as well as Lila, (has, have) stolen my heart.
5. There (happen, happens) to be a *ghost* in my attic.
6. *Anybody* who doesn't share my views (are, is) a Communist.
7. *Each* of these planes (flies, fly) faster than the speed of sound.
8. The *number* of dogs in the alley (are, is) increasing.
9. There (don't, doesn't) seem to be any *cookies* in this jar.

10. A *portion* of the profits (are, is) yours.
11. Skillful *gymnastics* (require, requires) a high degree of limber body control.
12. At the end of the semester, there (is, are) *exams* and *dorm checkout*.
13. A *number* of library books (go, goes) astray each year.
14. *Everybody* (has, have) answers but *nobody* (has, have) questions.
15. These days, the *news* (depress, depresses) everybody.

18 Pronoun References I: Agreement

Pronouns sometimes refer back to a word or group of words called *antecedents*. You can be sure your pronouns and antecedents will agree if you follow these rules.

1. In referring to persons, places, and things, use pronouns that agree in person and number.

Tom told me about *his* troubles; *he* seemed very upset.
The *plane* lifted *its* nose and rose in the air.
The *Democrats* will nominate a liberal; *they* always do.

2. Use singular pronouns in referring to antecedents like these: *any, anybody, anyone, each, every, everybody, everyone, either, neither, man, woman, person, nobody, none, someone, somebody*. In informal writing, plural pronouns refer to some of these, but for formal writing use the singular.

Informal   Everybody knows *their* dreams.
Formal   Everybody knows *his* dreams.

3. In the case of a collective noun used as an antecedent, use a singular pronoun if you are thinking of the group as a unit, or a plural pronoun if you are thinking of the members separately.

The committee made *its* decision.
The committee shared *their* opinions with the press.

4. When two or more antecedents are joined by *and*, *nor*, or *or*, the following rules apply: (A) When two or more antecendents are joined by *and*, use a plural pronoun; (B) when two or more singular antecedents are joined by *or* or *nor*, use a singular pronoun; (C) when one of the antecedents joined by *or* or *nor* is singular and the other plural, use a pronoun that agrees with the nearest of the two.

A. *Jason and Scott* did *their* best work after lunch.
B. Neither *Jason nor Scott* has *his* car this weekend.
C. Neither the *director nor the actors* are ready for *their* opening night.

18 Exercise/PRONOUN ANTECEDENT AGREEMENT

Make all the pronouns in the following sentences agree with their antecedents according to the principles of formal usage.

1. Neither Nina nor Natalie knows their uncle very well.

2. The conductor raised his baton and the band raised its instruments to play.

3. If a restaurant or a disco opened in our neighborhood, they would do a great business.

4. By winning on Sunday, the team raised their record to 7-0.

5. Every woman should have a right to their own body.

6. Either James or Paul does their homework on Sunday.

7. The orchestra carried its own instruments into the hall.

8. Neither Dennis nor Jackie insists that their money be invested.

9. Everybody has their feelings.

10. The Senate did their work in private.

11. Neither the captain nor the sergeant could make up their minds.

12. Either my mother or my sisters are always worrying about her clothes.

13. Sam and Richard attended to his cats.

14. A tennis player should try to develop their serve.

15. The sun and the moon cast its light in all directions.

16. Each player has their own style.

17. The Congress decided to raise the pay of their members.

18. Neither the professors nor the student paid their own way.

19. Everyone in the stands felt the heat of the sun on their body.

20. A doctor must decide what is best for their patients.

21. The members of the labor union needed to establish its working hours.

19 Pronoun References II: Ambiguity

In the heat of composition, writers can fail to notice that they are using a pronoun ambiguously, that is, using it in such a way that the reader has trouble identifying the antecedent of the pronoun. The following rules may be used as guides to eliminate these uncertainties.

1. Do not use pronouns that can refer back to more than one antecedent.

Ambiguous Donna reminded Lisa that *her* rent was due. (Whose rent?)
Clear Donna reminded Lisa that Lisa's rent was due. *Or* Lisa was reminded that Donna's rent was due.
Ambiguous When James looked at his father, *he* smiled. (Who smiled?)
Clear His father smiled, when James looked at him. *Or* When he looked at his father, James smiled.

2. Do not use a pronoun whose antecedent is remote from it, that is, too far away from the thing it refers to.

Remote The genius of men like Sigmund Freud reminds us of the human capacity to think, to imagine, and to erect a life's work on the ground of our mental efforts. *They* are amazing. (Not *mental efforts*, not the three parallel infinitive phrases, but *men like Sigmund Freud* are amazing.)
Revised The genius of men like Sigmund Freud is amazing; *it* [referring unmistakably, on the grounds of proximity, to *genius*] reminds us of the human capacity to think, to imagine, and to erect a life's work on the ground of our mental efforts.

3. Do not use pronouns with faulty broad reference. A pronoun with broad reference is one that refers back to a whole idea rather than a single noun or phrase. When such a pronoun refers back to more than one idea, we say that it has a faulty broad reference. The vague use of *this*, *that*, and *which* most frequently results in faulty broad references.

Faulty Broad Reference He bought a jazzy sportscar to make an impression on his girlfriend. *That* was not easy. (What was not easy: buying a car or making an impression on his girlfriend?)
Revised He bought a jazzy sportscar to make an impression on his girlfriend. *That purchase* was not easy. (Now things are clear. Frequently, a noun in the right place—after *that* or *this*—can do the job.)

Faulty Broad Reference He spent his time getting help with his income tax forms, *which* his wife considered unfair. (What does she consider unfair: the tax forms, that he spends his time on them, or that he gets help with them?)

Revised His wife considered it unfair that he spent his time getting help with his income tax forms. (We have had to recast the sentence to get rid of the *which* clause. Frequently, this is necessary.)

Remember that broad pronoun reference is not prohibited, only a faulty one. Sometimes, things are perfectly clear:

I'm taking a vacation. *That's* the only thing I care about.
We need to save money. *This* is the only way we can stay solvent.

4. Do not use pronouns with *implied antecedents*. That is, do not let the pronoun refer to a noun or a whole idea that is absent from the sentence. The vague use of *it, you, they,* and *them* frequently causes this error.

Implied Antecedent *It* says in my notebook that China is a socialist state. (Is there a talking *it* in the notebook?)

Revised *My notebook* says that China is a socialist state.

Implied Antecedent In some colleges, *you're* not allowed to dip below a 2.0 average.

Revised In some colleges, students are not permitted to dip below a 2.0 average.

Implied Antecedent *They* have mostly an agricultural economy in Southeast Asia.

Revised The economy in Southeast Asia is mostly agricultural.

Implied Antecedent I go to Yankee Stadium because I like to watch *them* play.

Revised I go to Yankee Stadium because I like to watch the Yankees play.

---

19 Exercise/PRONOUN REFERENCES: CATCHING THE AMBIGUITIES

Some of the sentences below have perfectly clear pronoun references. Next to these, place the letter *C*. Others, however, have ambiguous pronoun references of several types; correct these, even if you have to recast the sentences.

1. Mary saw Jean go into the store but she didn't realize it.

_____

_____

2. Jim and Susan wrote a piece for the college lit magazine. It wasn't very good.

_____

_____

3. The new curriculum passed by the faculty council shouldn't have included math. It's too much of a burden for the students.

_____

_____

4. He spent a lot of his time studying biology and preparing his dog for show trials, which his friends thought was weird.

_____

_____

5. They have a tightly knit society in China.

_____

_____

6. The college has an unbeaten football team. It's very proud.

_____

_____

7. He was involved with making money. That's all he cared about.

_____

_____

8. When Joe told his father the news, he smiled.

_____

_____

9. In Nebraska, they have all these cornfields.

_____

_____

10. Harry's new car was beautifully tuned, so he took us on a ride up into the mountains. It was wonderful.

11. The doctor said he was terribly run down. That scared him.

_____

_____

12. It says in college regulations that pets are not allowed in dormitory rooms.

_____

_____

13. George had a great deal of knowledge and used it to write a scholarly book. It was very detailed.

_____

_____

14. I went to the Mormon Tabernacle. I love to hear them sing.

_____

_____

15. He spent a lot of money getting advice about his divorce, which his friends thought futile.

_____

_____

16. In some discos, you're not allowed to drink liquor.

_____

_____

17. He dropped the statue on the glass coffee table and broke it.

_____

_____

18. He was trying to get elected to the student council so that he could do something constuctive about student complaints. This was not possible.

_____

_____

19. I want to study medicine. They are dedicated to saving human lives.

_____

_____

20. Linsey wrote her novel in longhand and Ingrid did a hunt and peck typing job with it. That was hard.

_____

_____

20 Verbs and Their Problems

The English verb is either regular, having *-d* or *-ed* forms in the past tense and the past participle, or irregular. Irregular verbs do not form their past and past participle forms in this way. Be careful to memorize irregular verb forms and to use the endings of regular verbs properly.

Regular verbs

Not   Yesterday they *play* basketball.
But   Yesterday they *played* basketball.

Irregular verbs

There are about 200 irregular verbs in English. The following is a list of the principal ones. Some of them you already know; you can check the principal parts of the others by consulting a dictionary.

Present (stem)	Past	Present Participle	Past Participle
arise	arose	arising	arisen
bear	bore	bearing	borne
begin	began	beginning	begun
bind	bound	binding	bound
blow	blew	blowing	blown
break	broke	breaking	broken
bring	brought	bringing	brought
buy	bought	buying	bought
catch	caught	catching	caught
choose	chose	choosing	chosen
come	came	coming	come
creep	crept	creeping	crept
deal	dealt	dealing	dealt
do	did	doing	done
draw	drew	drawing	drawn
drink	drank	drinking	drunk
drive	drove	driving	driven
eat	ate	eating	eaten
fall	fell	falling	fallen

Present (stem)	Past	Present Participle	Past Participle
flee	fled	fleeing	fled
fly	flew	flying	flown
forbid	forbade	forbidding	forbidden
forget	forgot	forgetting	forgotten
freeze	froze	freezing	frozen
get	got	getting	gotten
give	gave	giving	given
go	went	going	gone
grind	ground	grinding	ground
grow	grew	growing	grown
hang	hung*	hanging	hung*
hold	held	holding	held
hurt	hurt	hurting	hurt
know	knew	knowing	known
lay	laid	laying	laid
lead	led	leading	led
lend	lent	lending	lain
lie	lay	lying	lain
lose	lost	losing	lost
mean	meant	meaning	meant
mistake	mistook	mistaking	mistaken
ride	rode	riding	ridden
ring	rang	ringing	rung
rise	rose	rising	risen
run	run	running	run
see	saw	seeing	seen
seek	sought	seeking	sought
send	sent	sending	sent
shake	shook	shaking	shaken
shine	shone/shined	shining	shone/shined
sing	sang	singing	sung
sleep	slept	sleeping	slept
slide	slid	sliding	slid
speak	spoke	speaking	spoken
spin	spun	spinning	spun
spill	spilt/spilled	spilling	spilled
spit	spat	spitting	spat
spread	spread	spreading	spread
spring	sprang	springing	sprung
steal	stole	stealing	stolen
sting	stung	stinging	stung
stink	stank	stinking	stunk
strike	struck	striking	stricken/struck
swear	swore	swearing	sworn
swim	swam	swimming	swum
swing	swung	swinging	swung

*The past and past particple forms are *hanged* when the word is used in the sense of *executed*.

Present (stem)	Past	Present Participle	Past Participle
take	took	taking	taken
teach	taught	teaching	taught
tear	tore	tearing	torn
thrive	throve/thrived	thriving	thrived/thriven
throw	threw	throwing	thrown
wear	wore	wearing	worn
weep	wept	weeping	wept
win	won	winning	won
write	wrote	writing	written

Some of those that give trouble are *sit*, *set*, *lie*, *lay*, *lose*, and *loose*.

Lose means "to misplace" or "be unable to locate," whereas *loose* means to "set free" or "release." *Lose* is irregular (principal parts: *lose*, *lost*, *lost*); *loose* is regular.

To *sit* means to "rest with the torso supported at the buttocks." It is intransitive. To *set* means "to place down in some specified position." It is transitive. (Principal parts of *sit: sit, sat, sit;* principal parts of *set: set, set, set.*)

Lie and *lay* require special discrimination. *Lie* is intransitive; it means to "rest or recline in an incumbent position." Its principal parts are *lie, lay, lain.*

I *lie* here because I'm tired.
I *lay* there all afternoon.
I have *lain* here for hours.

Lay is transitive; it means to "put in a recumbent position." Its principal parts are *lay, laid, laid.*

He *lays* the package on the table.
She *laid* the baby in the crib.
She *had laid* the book on the desk.

Tenses

Here are the tenses of a regular verb, *to hear.*

INDICATIVE MOOD

Present Tense

ACTIVE VOICE

I hear	we hear
you hear	you hear
he, she, it hears	they hear

PASSIVE VOICE

I am heard	we are heard
you are heard	you are heard
he, she, it is heard	they are heard

Past Tense

ACTIVE VOICE

I heard	we heard
you heard	you heard
he, she, it heard	they heard

PASSIVE VOICE

I was heard	we were heard
you were heard	you were heard
he, she, it was heard	they were heard

Future Tense

ACTIVE VOICE

I will hear	we will hear
you will hear	you will hear
he, she, it will hear	they will hear

PASSIVE VOICE

I will be heard	we will be heard
you will be heard	you will be heard
he, she, it will be heard	they will be heard

Perfect Tense

ACTIVE VOICE

I have heard	we have heard
you have heard	you have heard
he, she, it has heard	they have heard

PASSIVE VOICE

I have been heard	we have been heard
you have been heard	you have been heard
he, she, it has been heard	they have been heard

Past Perfect Tense

ACTIVE VOICE

I had heard	we had heard
you had heard	you had heard
he, she, it had heard	they had heard

PASSIVE VOICE

I had been heard	we had been heard
you had been heard	you had been heard
he, she, it had been heard	they had been heard

Future Perfect Tense

ACTIVE VOICE

I will have heard	we will have heard
you will have heard	you will have heard
he, she, it will have heard	they will have heard

PASSIVE VOICE

I/you/he, she, it/we/you/they will have been heard

SUBJUNCTIVE MOOD

Present Tense

ACTIVE VOICE
that I/you/he, she, it/we/they hear
PASSIVE VOICE
that I/you/he, she it/we/they be heard

Past Tense

ACTIVE VOICE
that I/you/he, she, it/we/they heard
PASSIVE VOICE
that I/you/he, she, it/we/they were heard

Perfect Tense

ACTIVE VOICE
that I/you/he, she, it/we/they have heard
PASSIVE VOICE
that I/you/he, she, it/we/they have been heard.

Note: The past perfect tense is the same as the indicative forms.

Sequence of Tenses

When more than one verb is used in a sentence or in a pair of related sentences, the problem of *sequence of tenses* may arise. That is, it is important for the writer to specify with logic the time at which the action takes place or the state of being in force.

1. Be sure that the tenses of subordinate clauses are logically related.

Incorrect When Joe *entered* the room, he *sees* John.
Revised When Joe *entered* the room, he *saw* John.
  When Joe *enters* the room, he *sees* John.
Incorrect If he *tried,* he *could have gone* to graduate school.
Revised If *he had tried,* he *could have gone* to graduate school.

2. Use the present infinitive to indicate action that happens at the same time as or later than the action of the main verb, and use the present perfect infinitive (*to + have + * past participle) for action prior to that of the main verb.

George *wanted to leave.* George *wants* to leave.
He *would love to have given* more to the United Way. (The lost opportunity to *give* was prior to the verb *love.*)

3. Use the present participle to denote action happening at the same time as the main verb, and the present perfect participle (*having* + past participle of verb) for action prior to that of the main verb.

86

Looking through the telescope, he *saw* the moon. (*Looking* and seeing really take place at the same time.)

Having looked through the telescope, he knew it was a good one. (First comes the *looking*, then the *knowing*.)

Subjunctive Mood

The subjunctive is troublesome where the indicative and imperative are not. But the subjunctive mood is still important in the following circumstances.

1. In contrary-to-fact propositions:

If I *were* a rock star, I'd give free concerts.
He was eating as if there *were* nothing else on his mind.

2. In certain *that* clauses:

We suggest that you *be* prompt to the meeting.
He moved that the meeting *be* adjourned.
It is important that justice *be* done.

3. Where clarity is urgently needed:

I insist that the barn *be* painted red. (Note what happens to the meaning of the verb to indicative *is*.)

4. In certain idiomatic expressions:

Peace be with you.
Be that as it may.
Be it ever so humble, there's no place like home.
Far be it from me.

Final *-ed* or *-d*

Writers have to be careful to include in their written work all final *-d*'s and *-ed*'s. The problem here is that we have trouble hearing slurred regular past and past participle forms.

Auxiliary Verbs

The problems arise here mainly in these two places:

1. In the case of the *shall-will* pair, most American writers prefer to use *will* (plus the infinitive form without *to*) in all persons to form the future tense.

He *will go* to camp this summer.

However, some writers reserve *shall* for the first person and also use it to express forceful intentions in a somewhat stilted formal way.

We *shall* decide tomorrow.
You *shall* pay for that, young man!

2. Misuse of certain modal auxiliaries occur when the writer hears, for example, *could of* instead of the correct *could have* and writes the phrase that way. The same happens with *would, should, might, ought to.*

Incorrect He *should of* gone to bed.
Revised He *should have* gone to bed.

Would have is also misused in another way:

Incorrect If he *would have gone* to college, he would have been better prepared for the business world.
Revised If he *had gone* to college, he would have been better prepared for the business world.

---

20 Exercise/CORRECTING VERB PROBLEMS

A. Circle the form or forms appropriate to complete each of the following phrases.

Example   She could have   (try, (gone,) (waited,) making).

1. I was   (named, known, took, tried, waking, hang).
2. We had   (want, estimate, looking, broken, taken).
3. They must be   (joking, asking, rejected, taste, fool).
4. She will have   (asking, lose, lost, beat, shipped).
5. The stadium might have been   (filled, leaking, dome, close).
6. The situation could not have been   (help, changed, happening).
7. We will   (trying, soaking, look, went, argued).
8. They ought to have   (make, select, drive, hit, jump, suppose).
9. She had   (write, forgive, forgave, meant, aimed).
10. The building could not have been   (build, construct, locate, bought).

B. Fill in the blanks in the sentences given with the correct tense of the verb requested.

Example   The tournament will end soon and our team (lose)

___will have lost___ its chance for the championship.

88

1. When Bill (enter)_____ the room, he saw that Joanna

   (rearrange)_____ the furniture.

2. By the time you get to work, I (clean)_____ the whole house from top to bottom.

3. I (learn)_____ quite a bit of mathematics this year, and I hope to learn even more next year.

4. Fred was terrified that his dog (bite)_____ the police officer.

5. By the time my next birthday comes around, I (graduate)_____

   _____ from college.

6. Once I (finish)_____ my economics examination, I

   (begin)_____ to worry about my biology final.

7. The people we met on the beach (behave)_____ like clowns.

8. Before I found out about the Toyota, the Datsun (be)_____

   _____ my favorite car.

9. The chairman (leave)_____ the meeting before it

   (adjourn)_____ .

10. When the concert (end)_____ , the theater (close)

    _____ .

   C. Fill in the blanks with the correct forms of the irregular verbs in parentheses.

1. We were (lead)_____ into the room where the newly

   plastered ceiling had (fall)_____ .

2. We (lay)_____ the packages down on the countertop

   and (begin)_____ to get supper on the stove.

3. "What have you (do) _____ with the new slippers your

mother (buy) _____ me?" my father asked.

4. The fabric has been (weave) _____ from a special yarn

that was (mistake) _____ for cotton, even by experts.

5. Because he had (forget) _____ to send in his preregis-

tration form, Dennis was (forbid) _____ to attend
classes.

6. Eddie had (drink) _____ what seemed like quarts of

Alka-Seltzer before he could (lie) _____ down to nurse
his hangover.

   D. Write sentences in at least two tenses using the following troublesome
verbs.

   1. lie

   _____

   _____

   _____

   2. lay

   _____

   _____

   _____

   3. sit

   _____

   _____

   _____

4. set

_____

_____

_____

E. Correct each of the inappropriate verb forms you find in these sentences.

1. We should ought to see if we're suppose to register this week.

2. He could of gone to Buffalo this week like he use to.

3. This afternoon, Mike shall play the violin for us.

4. If he would have carry a spare tire with him, the flat wouldn't be such a disaster.

5. Being that he was just a kid, I helped him onto the swing.

6. He might of been a scholarship candidate if he would of study harder.

7. If he would have done well on his GRE's, he would have been admitted to graduate school.

8. They shall have coffee at the inn.

9. Raymond and Mary use to say that they wish they were back in Kansas.

10. First, he jump onto a chair and then he start singing "The Battle Hymn of the Republic."

F. Make sure the following sentences use the correct verb sequences by re-writing those that require it.

1. Teaching English, she thought she knew grammar.

_____

_____

2. Charley insisted that he once saw an acrobat do a triple somersault.

_____

_____

3. Being taught geometry, I can never forget the Pythagorean theorem.

_____

_____

4. Pamela plans to have married her fiancé next year.

_____

_____

5. They had not expected to have gone to France last summer.

_____

_____

6. Finishing the dessert, Colin walked away from the dinner table.

_____

_____

7. Bud regretted being born handsome instead of clever.

_____

_____

8. Arthur wanted to have taken the courses in sequence.

_____

_____

9. William thought Arthur missed the point, that he neglected the real issues.

_____

_____

10. When they have visited France, they never ate a bad meal.

_____

_____

21 Exercise/REVIEW TEST: SENTENCE FAULTS

Each of the following sentences commits one or another of the basic sentence faults we have been studying in this section. Correct all of them, even if you have to recast the sentence in order to do so.

1. Cornell has a College of Forestry, with a degree from there you can apply to the U. S. Department of Parks for an appointment.

   _____

   _____

2. Because I am much too young and inexperienced, I think it the better part of wisdom. Not to commit myself to a particular college major until I'm a junior.

   _____

   _____

3. Living alone in college dormitories are likely to present the student with many problems.

   _____

   _____

4. My mother gave my sister and I U. S. Savings Bonds for Christmas.

   _____

   _____

5. I like the smell of flowers; they pervade the whole room.

   _____

   _____

6. If she would have scored higher on the SAT's, she would have gotten into Harvard.

7. Finishing my homework, I decided it would be a good idea to go for a walk and get some air.

8. Every woman should have a right to their own body.

9. If a doctor or a lawyer opened an office in our neighborhood, they would soon have large practices.

10. Nobody ever thinks their troubles are their own fault, they always blame others.

11. Shelley had paid a fortune for the new set of dishes. Which was bound to anger her husband.

12. Economics are a difficult subject for a college freshman.

13. The man to who she gave her heart was from her home town.

_____

_____

14. It was an agreeable time of year, spring always is.

_____

_____

15. They fired two stockboys, Jim and I.

_____

_____

16. Neither my aunt nor my uncles plays bridge.

_____

_____

17. I enjoy going to Yankee Stadium because I love to see them play.

_____

_____

18. He engaged a small army of construction people to work on the remodeling of his house, which his friends thought was foolish.

_____

_____

19. The players—Frank, Tom, and me—were very excited as the game began.

_____

_____

20. Having been related to some of the most prominent families in the East. Joe knew the social scene very well.

_____

_____

Effective
Sentences

22 Subordination: Sentence Combining

In a sentence containing more than one idea, the least important should be subordinated to the most important. Ideas can be subordinated by casting them into subordinate clauses (using words like *after, although, which, who, that, because,* and the like), phrases (using participles), or single words.

My Uncle Bud was a professor *who specialized in literature.* (Subordinate idea is a dependent clause.)

My Uncle Bud was a professor *specializing in literature.* (Subordinate idea is a participial phrase.)

My Uncle Bud was a *literature* professor. (Subordinate idea is a single word.)

In subordinating, avoid the following pitfalls:

Subordinating the more important idea:

Whenever *I break into a cold sweat,* I take college exams.

Using the wrong subordinating conjunction:

I read in *Time where* Detroit is going to make only small cars. (*That* would be the correct choice.)

Using the primer style:

We were frightened. Our palms were sweaty. We heard a twig snap. We jumped. The moon came out suddenly. We ran.

Unless you wish to achieve a suspenseful effect, subordinate:

Because we were frightened, our palms were sweaty. *When* we heard a twig snap, we jumped, and as the moon came out, we ran.

22 Exercise/COMBINING SENTENCES AND REWRITING TO PRODUCE CLAUSES, PHRASES, AND WORDS

A. Combine each of the following groups of sentences into one or two effective ones using the techniques of subordination.

Examples   **1.** Juliet loved Romeo.
She believed Romeo was dead.
She took her own life.

Because Juliet loved Romeo, whom she believed was dead, she took her own life.

2. I'm taking a course.
It's a math course.
The course is taught by a woman.
She used to be a nun.

I'm taking a math course that's taught by a woman who used to be a nun.

Note: Not every student will combine the groups in exactly the same way. Several ways are possible.

1. I went to the newsstand this morning.
The *Tribune* was sold out.
I bought the *Post*.
I hate it.

_____

_____

_____

2. Chopin spent nearly twenty years in Paris.
Paris is the most cosmopolitan city in the world.
His music remained Polish.
His soul remained Polish.

_____

_____

_____

3. I spoke to your father on the telephone.
   It was Sunday night.
   He usually unnerves me.
   We had a very friendly chat.

   _____

   _____

   _____

4. I finished the book.
   My friend Debbie recommended it.
   I loved it.
   I always trusted her suggestions thereafter.

   _____

   _____

   _____

5. Ralph Waldo Emerson was an essayist and poet.
   He was American.
   He was also a Unitarian minister.
   He said, "To aim to convert a man by miracles is a profanation of the soul."

   _____

   _____

   _____

6. Jay Bergen is a lawyer.
   His office is on Park Avenue.
   He is with the firm of Marshall, Bratter, Green, Allison, & Tucker.
   He represents many illustrious clients.

   _____

   _____

   _____

101

7. Ice cream is fattening.
   I eat it all the time.
   I'm allowed to on my special diet.
   I made the diet up myself.

   _____

   _____

   _____

8. William Blake was a painter.
   He held imaginative vision above mere physical eyesight.
   He was a renowned poet.
   He was English.

   _____

   _____

   _____

9. The alarm rang.
   Tom opened his eyes.
   He saw the sun above the horizon.
   He knew it was getting late.

   _____

   _____

   _____

10. It snows.
    Children play happily outside.
    Many old people prefer to remain at home.
    They are afraid of slipping on the ice.

    _____

    _____

    _____

11. The lights came up.
    Lisa walked on stage.

The audience cheered.
The audience had waited on line for hours to buy tickets.

_____

_____

_____

12. The Phillies took the 1980 title.
They had never won a World Series before.
The Philadelphia fans went crazy.
Their dream had come true.

_____

_____

_____

B. Revise the following sentences through the effective use of subordination.

1. April wants to make a grand entrance so she arrives late.

_____

_____

2. I see that look on Barbara's face and I know something's wrong.

_____

_____

3. She was fascinated by parachute jumping and she didn't want to try it.

_____

_____

4. Donna wanted to get away from it all so she retreated to her villa on the Côte d'Azur.

_____

_____

5. I read too fast. I miss the important details.

_____

_____

6. The waiter brought me cold borscht and I didn't order it.

_____

_____

7. Ed was watching television but Maryanne was sewing.

_____

_____

8. Dinner was over so he cleared the dishes and crumbs from the table.

_____

_____

9. Rose is easily offended by harsh language so Peter watches his words.

_____

_____

10. Murphy likes the smell of garlic so he hangs around Lucia's kitchen.

_____

_____

11. I came home. The house was dark. I entered. The lights came on. My friends jumped up. They shouted surprise.

_____

_____

_____

12. I was waiting for the bus. I was becoming impatient. Suddenly I heard music. I turned around. I saw the saxophone player. The bus pulled up.

_____

_____

_____

23 Coherence I: Dangling Modifiers

A dangling modifier is a phrase or clause that either modifies no word in the sentence or refers to the wrong word. Recognize and correct the following types of dangling modifiers; they cause the sentence to lack *coherence*.

Dangling Participial Phrase *Smoking my cigar*, a fire engine came roaring around the corner.

Revised *As I was smoking my cigar*, a fire engine came roaring around the corner. (Now there is a person—I—in the sentence because the phrase has been made into a clause, one method of correcting these.)

or

Smoking my cigar, I saw a fire engine come roaring around the corner. (Now the person—I—has been placed in the main clause where the phrase can properly refer to it.)

Dangling Gerund Phrase *After drilling my tooth*, my cavity stopped aching. (The *cavity* didn't do the drilling.)

Revised *After the dentist drilled my tooth*, my cavity stopped aching. (The phrase is now a clause.)

or

After drilling my tooth, my dentist stopped my cavity from aching. (Now the phrase refers to *dentist*, the new subject of the main clause.)

Dangling Infinitive Phrase *To become a physician*, aptitude and hard work are needed. (A person is needed in the sentence.)

Revised To become a physician, *one* needs to have aptitude and to work hard.

Dangling Elliptical Clause *When fishing*, my hook is always baited.

Revised When fishing, *I* always bait my hook. (New subject of main clause, I, now agrees with omitted subject of the elliptical clause.)

or

When *I am* fishing, my hook is always baited. (Missing parts of elliptical clause are now supplied; sentence is correct.)

Note: Some verbal phrases do not modify any single portion of the main clause but rather the whole of the clause. These are called *absolute constructions* and are not dangling modifiers.

Service on the subway having been halted, we had to walk.
The air being hot and humid, we went swimming.

23 Exercise/CORRECTING DANGLING MODIFIERS

Below are sentences with dangling modifiers. Correct them according to the methods just discussed.

1. To become a good photographer, the camera must be used carefully.

   _____

   _____

2. Driving up the rock-strewn mountain, the tire went flat.

   _____

   _____

3. While taking a shower, Jerry pounded on my door.

   _____

   _____

4. Riding in a swiftly moving vehicle, the landscape becomes blurred.

   _____

   _____

5. To play the guitar well, practice is necessary.

   _____

   _____

6. In checking the records, the error became clear.

   _____

   _____

7. If potted, the chicken tastes better.

_____

_____

8. Crashing on the shore, I could hear the waves.

_____

_____

9. To become a movie star, talent and luck must come into play.

_____

_____

10. While treading water, the fish swam in lazy circles.

_____

_____

11. Coming home late, the house was dark.

_____

_____

12. To find out the facts, an encyclopedia must be consulted.

_____

_____

13. Listening to the concert, the Ramones seemed very funky.

_____

_____

14. When clean, I like to use the shower.

_____

_____

15. While hurrying to class, my briefcase dropped into a manhole.

_____

_____

16. After releasing the report, new data were supplied to the committee.

_____

_____

24 Coherence II: Misplaced Modifiers

A misplaced modifier is a modifying word, phrase, or clause that does not point clearly and directly to what it is supposed to modify. Recognize and correct the following kinds of misplacement.

Misplaced Word He *almost decided* to eat half the pie for supper.
Revised He decided to eat *almost half the pie* for supper.

Note: Other words of this type likely to be misplaced: *even, hardly, just, merely, only, scarcely.*

Misplaced Phrase My girl friend made it clear why we were breaking up *on Tuesday.*
Revised *On Tuesday*, my girl friend made it clear why we were breaking up.

Misplaced Clause The paint job is not dry *that they they did yesterday.*
Revised The paint job *that they did yesterday* is not dry.

A squinting modifier is a special type of misplacement referring both to what precedes and what follows it.

Squinting Modifier To be complimented *often* pleases a performer.
Revised It *often pleases* a performer to be complimented.

or

It pleases a performer *to be complimented often.*

---

24 Exercise/RECOGNIZING AND CORRECTING MISPLACED OR SQUINTING MODIFIERS

Correct the following misplaced or squinting modifiers.

1. She only liked cherry tomatoes.

_____

_____

2. The doll belongs to my sister whose head is missing.

_____

_____

3. She drove across the desert with a lump in her throat.

_____

_____

4. Professors who teach rarely get rich.

_____

_____

5. She got a job with Macy's after she had left school which lasted for more than fifteen years.

_____

_____

6. Arthur became panicked soon after he married and filed for divorce.

_____

_____

7. The professor told them when the class was over they could ask questions.

_____

_____

8. The mayor announced that he would run for reelection just last Friday.

_____

_____

9. The culprit only confessed when faced with proof of his crime.

_____

_____

10. The boat just docked here last week.

_____

_____

11. A baby was found abandoned in a snowsuit on Park Avenue.

_____

_____

12. George bought a pure Siamese from a friend that was already housebroken.

_____

_____

13. I boarded the train in the State of Connecticut that was heading south.

_____

_____

14. When he stopped reading suddenly they looked up.

_____

_____

15. They knew hardly what to do.

_____

_____

25 Coherence III: Split Constructions, Illogical Comparisons, Illogical Subjects or Complements, Illogical Omissions

Coherence can be maintained by avoiding the following illogical constructions:

Separating Subject and Verb

Poor *Alan,* in the middle of developing and printing an important roll of film, *took* the time to see that Maggie was all right.

Revised In the middle of developing and printing an important roll of film, *Alan took* the time to see that Maggie was all right.

Separating the Verb and Its Complement

Poor Emily *delivered,* having considered the matter in some detail, the *doll* to her brother Eli.

Revised Having considered the matter in some detail, *Emily delivered* the doll to her brother Eli.

Splitting an Infinitive

Poor We expected Shelley and Jim *to momentarily arrive.*

Revised We expected Shelley and Jim *to arrive momentarily.*

Note: Occasionally, it is appropriate to split the infinitive if *not* doing so would be awkward: *To just miss* the train was frustrating. Finlandia Cheese expects *to more than double* its business this year.

Using Illogical Subjects *Because he drove too fast* made us miss seeing the pretty countryside.

Revised Because he drove too fast, *we missed* seeing the pretty countryside.

or

Driving too fast, he made us miss seeing the pretty countryside.

Using Illogical Complements

Poor The thing that surprises me *is when* I can swim a mile without getting tired.
Revised It surprises me that I can swim a mile without getting tired.

Poor My favorite vacation *is where* I can relax at the seashore.
Revised My favorite vacation is relaxing at the seashore.

Using Mixed Comparisons

Poor My history professor is as interesting *if not more interesting* than my sociology professor. (The italicized phrase is misplaced, making the main clause read "My history professor is as interesting than my sociology professor.")
Revised My history professor is as interesting as my sociology professor, if not more interesting.
Revised (but stilted) My history professor is as interesting as, if not more interesting than, my sociology professor.

Using Inexact Comparisons

Poor Los Angeles is farther from Paris than New York. (Which place is farther from which?)
Revised Los Angeles is farther from New York than Paris *is.*

Using Incomplete Comparisons

Poor Her prospects for a job after graduation looked better than her brother.
Revised Her prospects for a job after graduation looked better than her brother's /or those of her brother/.

Omitting Words That Are Necessary to Maintain Parallel Structure

Poor We knew that she had talent but she lacked drive.
Revised We knew that she had talent but *that* she lacked drive.

Omitting Necessary Parts of Verbs

Poor Joanna *has* and always *will be* the most important woman in my life.
Revised Joanna *has been* and always *will be* the most important woman in my life.

Omitting Words Through Carelessness

Poor The prospects for women engineering are enormous.
Revised The prospects for women *in* engineering are enormous.

25 Exercise/RESTORING THE LOGIC TO ILLOGICAL CONSTRUCTIONS

Restore the logic to the following constructions by rewriting the sentences in which they appear.

1. Over the sink is where I hang my pots.

_____

_____

2. He was living and still does at the Evergreen Apartments.

_____

_____

3. A Volkswagen is built better and gets better gas mileage.

_____

_____

4. Stanford accepts more people from the West than others.

_____

_____

5. Heroism is when somebody risks his life to save another's.

_____

_____

6. The actor wanted, because he didn't trust the producer, a very long-term contract.

_____

_____

7. Jack is one of the best if not the best actors in the College Drama Society.

_____

_____

8. The leading lady's dress looked like a floozy.

_____

_____

9. The new paint job I did on my car cost far less than a professional.

_____

_____

10. The psychologist told her that she had a strong ego but she didn't believe in herself.

_____

_____

11. In Washington is the great Hirshhorn Museum and which attracts millions of art lovers every year.

_____

_____

12. The dentist said I was to only return to his office if the tooth continued to hurt.

_____

_____

13. A good movie is when the script stresses action.

_____

_____

116

14. Frenchmen are just as polite to visitors as Russia or Spain.

_____

_____

15. Happiness is when you achieve your goals.

_____

16. By having your teeth attended to can save you a lot of money.

_____

_____

17. Under the pillow is where I keep my Kleenex.

_____

_____

18. By treating patients with chemicals is inherently dangerous.

_____

_____

19. The thing I love most is when a good night's TV is scheduled.

_____

_____

20. He asked me to as quickly as possible arrange a meeting with the dean.

_____

_____

26 Parallel Construction I: Words, Phrases, Clauses

The advantage of parallel construction is that it permits a reader to assimilate a series of ideas because all are in the same grammatical form.

Words in Parallel Form Jackie *raised* her glass, *took* a sip, *wiped* her lips, and *smiled* into the mirror. (Parallel verbs.) She likes skiing, camping, and hiking. (Parallel nouns/participles.)

Phrases in Parallel Form *To work hard, to love well, to know the world*—these were Donna's ideals. (Parallel infinitive phrases.)

Clauses in Parallel Form *When the battle is won, when the earth is at peace, when men are equal under justice*, we may enjoy the fruits of humanity. (Parallel adverbial clauses.)

26 Exercise/CORRECTING FAULTY PARALLELISM

None of the following sentences are parallel in form. Rewrite each one, using the form of the italicized portion for the whole series.

> *Example* Chris liked the activity of basketball, eating pizza, and *to swim.* (Infinitive phrase.)

> *Rewritten in Parallel* Chris liked to play basketball, to eat pizza, and to swim. (All infinitive phrases.)

1. Andrew was employed as a chauffeur, but his other duties included *shopping*, to do the laundry, and take out the garbage.

   _____

   _____

   _____

2. At the age of thirteen months, James is exhibiting remarkable agility of movement, he comprehends complex ideas, and *aggressiveness of character.*

   _____

3. *When we're well rehearsed*, when our timing is precise, our singer is in good voice, we sound as good as any other band in the city.

_____

_____

_____

4. On their first date they were talking, *ate*, and drank for hours.

_____

_____

_____

5. *Playing with dolls*, sewing, and to do the dishes are activities that both little boys and little girls should be encouraged to do.

_____

_____

_____

6. If Susan continues to attack her teachers, damage school property, and *stealing from the other pupils*, she should be expelled.

_____

_____

_____

7. After you *take a bath* and washing your hair, you'll feel better.

_____

_____

8. Barbara had the mistaken notion that to be a good wife meant obedience, silence, and *to perform the routine domestic functions.*

_____

_____

_____

9. In the recording of popular music, the separate tasks of production, *arranging,* and to engineer are often performed by one person who is simply called the producer.

_____

_____

_____

10. Everyone hates washing, *to iron,* and fold their laundry, but my friend Gene actually buys new clothes when the ones he owns get dirty.

_____

_____

_____

11. John manages to hold a responsible position, *earn an impressive salary,* he's writing screenplays, and to raise two children.

_____

_____

_____

12. Are *marrying,* child-rearing, and to shop all there is to life?

_____

_____

_____

13. Tom, who tends bar at the local bistro, comes home exhausted after listening to *admissions of adultery*, confessions of love, and people telling him about adventures all night long.

_____

_____

_____

14. I want to sell my car because I don't like *to wait on gas lines*, getting stuck in traffic, or parking.

_____

_____

15. Ned thinks that *dressing*, to play, and sing like Billy Joel will make him an overnight rock sensation.

_____

_____

27 Parallel Construction II: and who/and which and the Correlative Pairs

Be sure to avoid faulty parallelism with *and who* or *and which* constructions or the correlative pairs: *either/or, neither/nor, not only/but also, both/or,* and *whether/or.*

Faulty He is Tom Barrett, a great guitarist *and who* is also a superb printmaker. (One noun phrase, one clause.)
Better He is Tom Barrett, a great guitarist and a superb printmaker. (Two adjective–noun phrases.)
Better He is Tom Barrett, who is a great guitarist and a superb printmaker. (Two clauses.)

Faulty She is not only *brilliant* but also *has wealth.* (Phrase *has wealth* is not parallel to adjective *brilliant.*)
Better She is not only brilliant but also wealthy. (Two adjectives are parallel.)

Faulty Neither your mother plays golf nor your father. (Clause *your mother plays golf* is not parallel to phrase *your father.*)
Better Neither your mother nor your father plays golf. (*Your mother* now parallel to *your father.*)

Faulty He couldn't decide whether he should sink or to swim. (Clause *he should sink* not parallel to infinitive *to swim.*)
Better He couldn't decide whether to sink or to swim. (Two infinitives now parallel.)

---

27 Exercise/CORRECTING FAULTY PARALLELISM WITH AND WHICH/AND WHO AND THE CORRELATIVE PAIRS

Some of the following sentences are correct. Next to these, mark the letter C. Revise the others to achieve parallel form.

Example
Incorrect She was beautiful and who had a dynamic personality.
Corrected She was beautiful and had a dynamic personality.

122

1. _____ Lizzie hates either doing the dishes or to cook.

_____

_____

2. _____ Janet Mary is not only a good student but also a good tennis player.

_____

_____

3. _____ Finley was fired from his job because he was both a liar and stealing.

_____

_____

4. _____ Neither breaking his leg, nor failing his exams has prevented Christopher from going dancing every night.

_____

_____

5. _____ Whether she goes to the movies or working late in the office, Debbie can't forget her troubles at home.

_____

_____

6. _____ The camera takes clear pictures and which is easy to use.

_____

_____

7. _____ She refuses either to go by bus or riding the subway.

_____

_____

8. _____ Tima can't decide whether she should live in New York or to go back to Istanbul.

_____

_____

9. _____ A finicky Italian sportscar, inconvenient to service and which costs more than I make in a year, would be a ridiculous purchase.

_____

_____

10. _____ April is either overweight or she starves herself.

_____

_____

11. _____ Ruth Gray is a painter, an actress, and who writes plays.

_____

_____

12. _____ He was young and who had a lot of ambition.

_____

_____

13. _____ She was a fashion model and who had many offers to do movies.

_____

_____

14. _____ Not only am I angry, but also sad.

_____

_____

15. _____ Whether listening to people's problems or preparing an elaborate Italian meal, Joanna is in her element.

28 Shifts

Writers need to be consistent in the point of view from which their sentences are written. When they are not, they can produce for the reader needless and distracting shifts in *tense, person, number, voice,* and *mood.*

Shift in Tense He *drives* his car to school and then *parked* it in the student lot. (Shift from present to past tense.)
Revision He *drove* his car to school and then *parked* it in the student lot.

Shift in Person When *somebody* catches a cold, *you* should stay in bed. (Shift from *somebody*, third person, to *you*, second person.)
Revision When *somebody* catches a cold, *she* [or *he*] should stay in bed.

Shift in Number After *one* graduates, *they* should be ready for a career. (Shift from singular *one* to plural *they*.)
Revision After *one* graduates, *he* [or *she*] should be ready for a career.

Shift in Voice After a lot of money *had been spent* on clothes, he *decided* he didn't like any of them. (Shift from passive *had been spent* to active *decided*.)
Revision After he *had spent* a lot of money on clothes, he *decided* he didn't like any of them.

Shift in Mood First, *start* the water boiling and then you *should peel* the potatoes. (Shift from imperative *start* to indicative *should peel*.)
Revision First *start* the water boiling, and then *peel* the potatoes.

---

28 Exercise/CORRECTING SHIFTS

A. Some of the following sentences are correct: They show no shift in tenses. Next to these, write C. Rewrite the others to correct shifts in verb tense.

Example I *work* as a delivery boy and I *earned* a good salary.
Revised I *worked* as a delivery boy and I *earned* a good salary.

1. When I tell her that she's beautiful, she was happy.

_____

_____

2. I close the door because I needed to be left alone.

_____

_____

3. Bill wants to study medicine but he hated the prospect of four more years of school.

_____

_____

4. I took the money and I run.

_____

_____

5. We ate at the best restaurants and we paid the highest prices.

_____

_____

6. Dean arrived at the party and he has to be the center of attention.

_____

_____

7. When I brushed my teeth and then drink orange juice, I always regret it.

_____

_____

8. Ed runs twelve miles a day and hoped to qualify for the Olympics.

_____

_____

9. George strangled his mother and stuffed her body into the closet.

_____

_____

10. He adjusts the antenna and then changed the channel.

_____

_____

B. Some of the following sentences are correct: They show no shift in person. Next to these, write *C*. Rewrite the others to correct shifts in person.

> *Example* *She* never studied, and *you* can't do that without getting bad grades.
>
> *Revised* *She* never studied, and *one* can't do that without getting bad grades.

1. When somebody catches a praying mantis, you shouldn't kill it.

_____

_____

2. A psychiatrist will help you, but they will demand an exorbitant fee.

_____

_____

3. If a man is married, they shouldn't flirt with other women.

_____

_____

4. Anyone can learn Swahili if they will only try.

_____

_____

5. After one is under water for ten minutes, he will have difficulty breathing.

_____

_____

6. If you adhere strictly to the Jewish dietary laws, one can't eat baked ham.

_____

_____

7. When attending the opera, one should always remain in his seat until the intermission.

_____

_____

8. If we will examine the label carefully, you will see that this product contains additives.

_____

_____

9. I can never find a telephone booth when you need one.

_____

_____

10. If one perseveres, he will surely succeed.

_____

_____

C. Some of the following sentences are correct: They show no shift in number. Next to these, write C. Rewrite the others to correct shifts in number.

> Example   Our *society* should provide better care for *their* senior citizens.
>
> Revised   Our *society* should provide better care for *its* senior citizens.

1. A sensitive musician will listen carefully to their fellow members in the orchestra.

_____

_____

2. He was arrested for concealing a dangerous weapon on their person.

_____

_____

3. I think a person should mind their own business.

_____

_____

4. The gay community is struggling to maintain their voice in government.

_____

_____

5. Linda and Bobby must wait his turn to ride on the back of Uncle Joey's motorcycle.

_____

_____

6. They couldn't understand why their son moved to India.

_____

_____

7. A single mother needs a lot of help raising their children.

_____

_____

8. He couldn't afford his wife's taste for expensive jewelry.

_____

_____

9. Teachers have it easy, because his hours are short.

_____

_____

10. A daughter often takes after her mother.

_____

_____

29 Emphasis

1. The end of a sentence is the most emphatic position. Material placed there makes the greatest impact on a reader. The next most emphatic position is the beginning, and the middle of the sentence usually receives the least emphasis. Effective writing is that which achieves force through the careful use of the most emphatic positions.

Unemphatic   He has no chance of recovery, as the doctor sees it.
Stronger   As the doctor sees it, he has no chance of recovery.

Unemphatic   The history of public taste is the history of change, in many ways.
Stronger   The history of public taste is, in many ways, the history of change.

2. Writers can affect how they achieve emphasis by becoming aware of the *loose* and the *periodic* sentence. The loose sentence places its main idea first and its subordinate details afterward. The periodic sentence is constructed on the opposite principle: A series of subordinate details leads up to a main idea. The judicious use of the periodic, then, will permit the writer to achieve a certain amount of withheld suspense and drama.

Loose   The freshman student staggers through the first year, burdened with a strange environment, the loss of friends, and a difficult academic load.
Periodic   Burdened with a strange environment, the loss of old friends, and a difficult academic load, the freshman student staggers through the first year.

---

29   Exercise/ACHIEVING EMPHATIC SENTENCES

A. To make the following sentences more emphatic, rewrite them by altering the position of groups of words.

1. We're having fish for dinner whether he likes it or not.

_____

_____

2. Barbara's forehand and serve have improved, to a certain extent.

_____

_____

3. I'd like to get a written estimate beforehand, if possible.

_____

_____

4. You should buy clothes that are going to wear well, as a rule.

_____

_____

5. He did hand in all of his final papers, although late.

_____

_____

6. I'll order a bottle of red wine, unless someone objects.

_____

_____

7. Sol is a very sick man I think.

_____

_____

8. The guests were having such a fine time, they didn't want to leave, in spite of the late hour.

_____

_____

9. What makes Tom think he's better than the rest of us, I'd like to know.

_____

_____

10. Dirk is the best illustrator the magazine ever hired, in my judgment.

_____

_____

11. He showed no sign of recovery day after day.

_____

_____

12. You can't get good ribs outside of Chicago, according to some.

_____

_____

13. This election will be a landslide, in my opinion.

_____

_____

14. Peter is very much like his brother Cristoffer, in many ways.

_____

_____

15. The results of the test marketing were disappointing, by and large.

_____

_____

B. Rewrite the following loose sentences into periodic ones.

1. My grandfather was finally able to send for his family in Russia after traveling to this country alone and working in a factory for two years.

_____

_____

2. Debbie broke down and cried, hearing that music and remembering how things used to be.

_____

_____

3. The force of the wind shattered my bedroom window several years ago in the middle of a stormy night.

_____

_____

4. She will never speak to you again even if you apologize and send her a dozen red roses.

_____

_____

5. Three miles of beautiful mountain roads lay between our house and the nearest village.

_____

_____

6. Anton was disillusioned about romance after marrying young and undergoing a traumatic divorce.

_____

_____

7. Chris went for a walk, totally unaware of how cold it was outside, and wearing only a thin jacket.

_____

_____

8. We will name her Lucia, if, as we are hoping, the baby is a girl.

_____

_____

9. She made just enough money for her tuition and living expenses working as a waitress and selling homemade pies to a local restaurant.

_____

_____

10. Fred always won and only bet on horses with Italian names.

_____

_____

11. Judy and Lila cautiously crossed the street after the bus roared by, leaving a trail of smoke and exhaust.

_____

_____

12. An agreement was reached and the workers went back to their jobs after negotiations had gone on for two weeks.

_____

_____

13. She looks like royalty whether she wears jeans or an evening gown.

_____

_____

14. Annie couldn't give up cigarettes despite acupuncture treatments, hypnosis, and psychotherapy.

_____

_____

15. I am overdrawn in my account, according to my bank statement.

_____

_____

30 Sentence Length and Variety

Variation in the length and variety of the sentences you use will help to avoid monotony and achieve emphatic, interesting work. To acquire the liveliness of style that comes with varying one's sentence patterns, you should *first avoid the following:*

1. *The "primer" style.* This consists of short, choppy, declarative sentences, reminiscent of the sentences produced by young children.

Primer Style   The sun came up. We walked to work. We hummed a little tune.
Revised   As the sun came up, we walked to work, humming a little tune.

Primer Style   We saw a man. He was fat. He ate a lot. He didn't seem to care.
Revised   The man we saw was fat because he ate a lot, but he didn't seem to care.

Note that in the primer style, connections between ideas are missing. In the revisions, these relations are restored and the ideas are smoothly and logically connected.

2. *Long, excessively compounded sentences.* These are sentences that join together, willy-nilly, a number of independent clauses using *and* or other coordinating conjunctions.

Excessive Compounding   While Donald was swimming, I thought I noticed a shark in the water, and I called the lifeguard, but he was busy talking to some pretty girls and he didn't hear me, so I decided to take the lifeboat out myself.
Revised   While Donald was swimming, I thought I noticed a shark in the water. Although I called the lifeguard, he didn't hear me because he was talking to some pretty girls. In a panic, I decided to take the lifeboat out myself. (The third and fourth independent clauses have been turned into subordinate clauses. A phrase has been added to introduce the final independent clause.)

Using the same word order (subject-verb) in every sentence, and using the same type of sentence one after another (say the declarative type), contributes to monotony. The following techniques can help you achieve a desired level of variety:

1. Vary the beginning of your sentences.

The same basic sentence can be written in a variety of ways.

Sentence
The players practiced purposefully in the sun and they were unaware of the commotion in the stadium.

137

Varieties

Practicing purposefully in the sun, the players were unaware of the commotion in the stadium. (Begins with a verbal phrase.)

In the sun, the players practiced purposefully, unaware of the commotion in the stadium. (Begins with a prepositional phrase.)

Because the players practiced purposefully in the sun, they were unaware of the commotion in the stadium. (Begins with an adverb clause.)

There were players practicing purposefully in the sun, unaware of the commotion in the stadium. (Begins with an expletive.)

2. Reverse the usual order of subject-verb or subject-verb-object. To do this is to create a distinctly emphatic order and you should do so only where your aim is to achieve such emphasis.

Subject-Verb Order	Verb-Subject Order
The crowd marched to the game.	To the game marched the crowd.
Joe's dog rested in the shade.	In the shade rested Joe's dog.

Subject-Verb-Object Order	Object-Subject-Verb Order
Joanna loves swimming in the ocean.	Swimming in the ocean Joanna loves.
I never see Larry.	Larry I never see.

3. Occasionally, use a question or a command instead of a declarative sentence, but only when it is appropriate to do so.

Imperative (command) *Look* carefully at the steep decline of the American economy at the end of the 1970s.

Question What will happen to our children if we abdicate from our positions of parental authority? What will happen to us?

---

30 Exercise/REVISING FOR LENGTH AND VARIETY IN SENTENCES

A. Revise the following groups of short sentences by supplying connections between them.

1. I was a freshman. The school was very big. I couldn't make friends in the dorm. The professors didn't know my name. The year was frightening.

---

2. The car was new. The brakes didn't work. The paint job had bumps. I tried calling the dealer. He wouldn't listen. I had to call Detroit.

_____

_____

_____

3. I needed money. I asked Fred. I asked Ed. Nobody had any. Nobody cared. I remembered my mother, I called her.

_____

_____

_____

4. We went to the beach. It was hot. We couldn't walk on the sand. We went in the water. We came out. The sun dipped. We could walk.

_____

_____

_____

5. It was Tuesday. Al discovered he had a skin rash. It grew worse. On Friday, he went to the doctor. The doctor prescribed salve. He applied it on Saturday. By Tuesday, the rash had cleared up.

_____

_____

_____

B. Revise the following poorly joined groups of independent clauses by subordinating the less important ideas.

1. I didn't pass the final exam and I failed the course.

_____

2. The disco on Main Street used to be the police station, but now it's a major attraction for the young people in town and there are so many cars parked outside on Friday nights that traffic jams are created.

3. Fleetwood Mac has made many gold records and played concerts in dozens of foreign countries and is famous all over the world and is a special favorite of American teenagers.

4. James's uncle was a government official and lived in Mississippi and had moved to Washington in 1974.

5. Susan bought her new dress a few months ago and she has already worn it to three proms.

6. Kurt Vonnegut has lectured at many colleges and he has written twelve novels and he has also published his memoirs.

_____

_____

7. It was raining and we didn't go to the beach and we went to the movies.

_____

_____

_____

8. Members of the Student Council are really dedicated people and they give much of their study time to improving college living conditions, but the rest of the campus doesn't appreciate them enough and they often feel bitter because of this.

_____

_____

_____

_____

_____

9. The car was all loaded and we were ready to leave but I had left my fishing rod inside the house and I ran back to get it and I came back outside and everybody made remarks about me.

_____

_____

_____

_____

10. Roller skating is a new and popular pastime in America and many would

rather be on roller skates wearing a set of earphones than do anything else but the experience is isolating and to some it's also annoying.

_____

_____

_____

_____

_____

C. Revise the following sentences by changing beginnings. In some cases, it would also be appropriate to play with a reversed word order.

1. They returned from the beach sunburned and cranky after fighting the crowds all afternoon.

_____

_____

2. George went to the professor's office to protest the grade he'd received.

_____

_____

3. The billsticker, his arms full of paper and brushes, spread and stuck on the poster with extraordinary speed.

_____

_____

4. He knew his cold was getting worse because his head felt hotter and he could hardly breathe through his nose.

_____

_____

5. They wanted to make a cake and the mixer was broken.

_____

_____

6. She had lost her sense of purpose but was brought back to the true way by a magazine article she read.

_____

_____

7. Spring flooding caused much loss of livestock and crops in the valley of the Ohio River, and the federal government quickly offered assistance.

_____

_____

_____

8. They stayed only at youth hostels or slept overnight in friendly farmers' barns, which saved them a great deal of money, and they were able to make the tour at a relatively low cost.

_____

_____

_____

9. Inflation has debased the value of our dollars, and it is much more expensive to live in the United States than it used to be.

_____

_____

_____

10. He had lost the keys to his apartment, and he began to ask to see if anybody had found them.

_____

_____

_____

31 Exercise/REVIEW TEST: EFFECTIVE SENTENCES

Each of the sentences below violates some principle of making effective sentences. Rewrite each to eliminate the problem.

1. Having been pickled in formaldehyde for two weeks, our biology instructor handed us the specimens to dissect.

_____

_____

2. Over the fence is where I hit the home run.

_____

_____

3. While it rained in the morning, I couldn't take a walk.

_____

_____

4. She borrowed a bicycle from Ellen with ten speeds.

_____

_____

5. Karl's study habits and grades have improved, to a certain extent.

_____

_____

6. On the morning he wanted to leave turned out to be a Sunday.

_____

_____

7. He liked jogging, to make model airplanes, and listen to records.

_____

_____

8. Charley won the race; Fred was the better runner.

_____

_____

9. He took a sip. It tasted bitter. He spat it out.

_____

_____

10. Ed goes to school on the bus every morning, but he hated the crowds.

_____

_____

11. We repeated the same routine, day after day.

_____

_____

12. Bud was doing calisthenics and the others sitting around.

_____

_____

13. When he stopped crying pitifully they looked at him.

_____

_____

14. On the plane that night, they were talking, sang, and drank for hours.

_____

_____

15. She looked sick. I told her to go home.

_____

_____

16. The lights suddenly went out and we lit candles.

_____

_____

17. I can never find a police officer when you need one.

_____

_____

18. Traveling in circles, I saw the rudderless boat.

_____

_____

19. A lawyer will give you good professional advice, but they charge you a fortune for it.

_____

_____

20. His violin teacher told him frequently to practice.

_____

_____

Effective
Paragraphs
and
Compositions

32 The Paragraph: Unity and the Topic Sentence

Paragraphs are composed of sentences that relate to a central idea. More often than not, this central idea will be located in what we call the *topic sentence*. When all the sentences in a paragraph relate to the topic sentence, we say that the paragraph has *unity*. When they do not, we say that the paragraph lacks unity, one of the three criteria that mark every adequately written paragraph. (The other two are *coherence* and *adequate development*. See Sections 33 and 34.)

The topic sentence, it is thus easy to see, is what the paragraph is *about*. The other sentences do what is necessary to further illustrate, define, explain, analyze, or describe the main idea embodied in the topic sentence.

32 Exercise/MAKING UNIFIED PARAGRAPHS

A. Below are four paragraphs. In each, the topic sentence is italicized. Each of the other sentences in the paragraph is preceded by a number in brackets. Read through each paragraph and in the blanks that follow each, place the number or numbers of those sentences that do not relate to the topic sentence and cause the paragraph to lack unity.

Example

[1] *Burglars and robbers who commit a crime for the first time should not be sent to prison.* [2] Instead, they should be put on probationary programs. [3] I once knew a probation officer who did very good work. [4] Of all criminals, first offenders have the best chance of changing their ways. [5] Some have just been tipped over into the criminal life, and with the help of probationary programs, could be helped to see that noncriminal solutions to life's crises are possible. [6] After all, many people are under great stress and not all commit crimes. [7] On the other hand, to send first offenders to prison is to send them to great educational centers— for advanced training in criminality. [8] In prison, a first offender comes into contact only with hardened professionals. [9] On probation, he will be in contact with a law-abiding probation officer. [10] With which teacher would he therefore receive a better education in being a good citizen? 3, 6

1. [1] *There are several reasons why Americans are overweight.* [2] One of these is overeating. [3] Studies have shown that Americans take in 750 calories more each day than they actually need. [3] Famous heavyweights like Orson Welles eat god knows how much. [4] Moreover, most Americans—despite the recent consciousness of the importance of fitness—lead sedentary lives and rarely work off much of what they eat. [5] Of course, we all envy those skinny people who eat and eat and eat and never gain an ounce. [6] In addition, a surprising number of us are overweight because of glandular deficiencies of which we are unaware. [7] Probably the greatest reason we are overweight is our addiction to certain foods: high calorie fast foods like pizza, hamburgers, soft drinks, and sugary snacks. [8] The Chinese are lucky not to be exposed to foods like these. [9] Only educational programs, informing us of these dangers in our diet and fitness habits, can make us conscious of how overweight we are. _____

2 [1] *The condition of slavery was undeniably degrading to the black.* [2] In being constantly forced to do another's bidding, the slave was denied the opportunity to follow his own initiative and to develop self-discipline. [3] Any adolescent will tell you how much these things mean to his development. [4] No slave could gain the sense of responsibility and dignity that comes with caring for the self, owning a home or other significant property, and determining one's chosen work. [5] The slave was also denied an education because the educated have ideas and these lead to dissatisfaction with one's lot. [6] Being a slave was boring. [7] Denied all these opportunities for self-enhancement, the slave must have felt his personal degradation keenly. _____

3. [1] *Summer jobs can be crucial to a college student's development.* [2] Of course, the best of these jobs are not easy to get. [3] To get a well-paying and interesting summer job requires the student to exercise important skills such as résumé writing, making contact with employers and undergoing interviews, and undertaking a disciplined survey of a field. [4] Once in a job, the student is forced to experience real working conditions. [5] He needs to practice concentration, interpersonal relations, alertness to opportunity, and a whole host of other good work habits. [6] If he doesn't, he can easily be replaced: Dozens of others are waiting in the wings. [7] Moreover, if the student is lucky enough to get a summer job in his field, he can frequently gain important knowledge useful to his career. [8] Of course, working over the whole summer vacation can tire one out for the long haul of the new academic year. [9] Finally, the money earned in a summer job can contribute to a student's education and give him the sense of fulfillment that comes with earning one's way. _____

4. [1] *Old-fashioned sources of energy are becoming important again.* [2] People shouldn't look down their noses at things that are old-fashioned just because they're old. [3] The windmill is one of these because, in certain parts

of the country, where a constant wind of ten miles per hour is part of the weather pattern, it is the most economical source of power. [4] It is also important that the windmill does not pollute. [5] The landscape, with these bladed beauties turning lazily in the sun, would be beautiful again. [6] Another newly important source is the waterfall. [7] The waterfall also provides cheap power possibilities and does not pollute. [8] Many waterfalls were dammed up to provide recreational facilities in a man-made lake. [9] Of course, the oldest of all, the sun, is just beginning to be newly exploited in a hundred ways. _____

5. [1] *Television has had a number of bad effects on its viewers.* [2] Probably no more than a handful of Americans have no access to a TV set. [3] One of the worst effects is that too much television viewing isolates us from each other: We do not talk much to one another because we are too busy being absorbed in TV. [4] Furthermore, young people brought up on TV have lost or rather never gained good reading skills and are uninterested in books. [5] It's nevertheless amazing that TV talk shows are always plugging books. [6] Too much violence on TV leads, according to some experts, to antisocial behavior. [7] And some experts even think it leads to obesity because we all eat so much while we watch. [8] Even TV news shows are biased in the way they look at public events. _____

   B. Below are a number of topic sentences. Follow up each by writing in the blanks provided the next sentence that would follow if you were using the topic sentence to write a unified paragraph.

   Example
   A compact foreign car has many advantages over its larger domestic rivals.

   First, it costs much less to buy the foreign compact. _____

1. The business of American agriculture is in part subsidized by the American taxpayer.

   _____

   _____

   _____

2. Baseball players these days are worth the huge salaries they are being paid.

   _____

3. To take good photographs, the photographer must make a series of thoughtful choices.

_____

_____

4. Jogging is an important aid to overall physical fitness.

_____

_____

5. Nowadays, Americans are very nostalgic for "the old days."

_____

_____

6. On this campus, blue jeans are a uniform.

_____

_____

_____

7. Roller skating has become an important part of our national recreational habits.

_____

8. Overpopulation is one of the most serious problems facing world leaders today.

_____

_____

_____

9. Good study habits are the most important things a freshman can bring to college.

_____

_____

10. Television documentaries are the only things worth watching in the medium.

_____

_____

33 The Paragraph: Coherence

The second criterion for an effective paragraph is *coherence*. A *coherent* paragraph must (1) have some principle of order dictate the order in which each sentence follows the preceding one; and (2) the sentences in the paragraph must have clear connections between them: The connections may be of word, idea, or special phrase.

1. The subject of a paragraph will usually suggest the proper principle of order. Two common plans are the *chronological* and the *spatial*. The former is suitable for such subjects as a short narrative or sketch, where events can be placed in a time order. The latter is suitable for the description of a place or a large physical object. There, the spatial order can dictate an approach from the outside to the inside, from up to down, from far to near, and so forth.

Chronological
We had a number of close calls that day. When we rose, it was obviously late and we had to hurry so as not to miss breakfast; we knew the dining room staff was strict about closing at nine o'clock. Then, when we had been driving in the desert for nearly two hours—it must have been close to noon—the heat nearly did us in; the radiator boiled over and we had to use most of our drinking water to cool it down. By the time we reached the mountain, it was four o'clock and we were exhausted. Here, judgment ran out on us and we started the tough climb to the summit, not realizing that darkness came suddenly in the desert. Sure enough, by six we were struggling and Andrew very nearly went down a steep cliff, dragging Muhammad and me along with him. By nine, when the wind howled across the flat ledge of the summit, we knew as we shivered together for warmth that it had not been our lucky day.

Spatial
From a distance, it looked like a skinny tube, but as we got closer, we could see it flesh out before our eyes. It was tubular, all right, but fatter than we could see from far away. Furthermore, we were also astonished to notice that the building was really in two parts: a pagoda sitting on top of a tubular one-story structure. Standing ten feet away, we could marvel at how much of the pagoda was made up of glass windows. Almost everything under the wonderful Chinese roof was made of glass, unlike the tube that it was sitting on, which only had four. Inside, the tube was gloomy, because of the lack of light. Then a steep, narrow staircase took us up inside the pagoda and the light changed dramatically. All those windows let in a flood of sunshine and we could see out for miles across the flat land.

2. To assure that there are clear connections between your sentences, keep the following considerations in mind:

A. Present your ideas from a consistent point of view. Avoid needless shifts in tense, number, or person.

Shift in Tense
In the movie, Robert Redford was a spy. He goes to his office where he found everybody dead. Other spies *wanted* to kill him, so he *takes* refuge with Julie Christie. At her house, he *had waited* for the heat to die down, but they *come* after him anyway.

Shift in Number
Everybody looks for satisfaction in his life. *They* want to be happy. But if *he* seeks only pleasure in the short run, the *person* will soon run out of pleasure and life will catch up to him. *They* need to pursue the deeper pleasure of satisfaction in work and in relationships.

Shift in Person
Now more than ever *parents* need to be in touch with their children's activities because modern life has the tendency to cause cleavages in the family. *You* need to arrange family life so that members will do things together and know one another. *You* need to give up isolated pleasures of *your* own and realize that *parents* have a set of obligations to sponsor togetherness and therefore sponsor knowledge.

B. Use parallel construction in sentences that follow each other for the purpose of presenting parallel or coordinate ideas.

My mother has passed along to me certain rules for getting along with others. Don't argue with parents; they'll think you don't love them. Don't argue with children; they'll think themselves victimized. Don't argue with spouses; they'll think you're a tiresome mate. Don't argue with strangers; they'll think you're not friendly. My mother's rules, in fact, can be summed up in two words: Don't argue.

(See 26 Parallel Construction I., pp. 118–121, for more on this topic.)

C. Repeat key words and phrases to keep before the reader the flow of your thought. Pronouns referring to an antecedent are also useful for this purpose.

A *magic show works* by carefully *directing* our *attention*. But the *show directs* our *attention* where the *magician* wants it to be. *He* wants us to *look* away from the *place* where *his* transformations go on. For that *place* has no *magic*; it's a *work place*. The *magical* quality of the *show* depends on our not *seeing* the *work*. When *we* do not *look* at that *work*, we *see* the *magic*, and our *attention*—focused on the right *place*—is well rewarded.

D. Use *transitional devices* where they are necessary to further the function of bridging the gap between sentences. A *transitional* device is a word or phrase that can serve as a point of reference (*finally, at* *last*) or that actually can indicate the relationship between one sentence and another (*consequently, as a result*).

Soon he was able to hit the ball over the net more often than into the net. *Then* he began to practice every day, stroking hundreds of tennis balls all over the court. *Consequently*, he was able to hit shots with topspin and his backhand began to improve. *However*, his serve was still weak and he could only rarely get one into the service area. More practice followed; he just never tired of self-improving exercise. *Finally*, as the summer drew to a close, he felt he could play like a disciplined amateur.

---

33 Exercise/ACHIEVING COHERENT PARAGRAPHS

A. Below are sets of sentences identified by roman numerals. Next to each numeral is a sentence with which to begin a paragraph. Using the sentences that follow, construct coherent paragraphs, employing some logical plan of order, either chronological or spatial.

I. *Begin with:* The novelist James Joyce was born in Dublin, Ireland, in 1882.

1. Joyce's father was one of these—a speaker, singer, and storyteller—and very soon young James began to take after him.
2. Later on, he wrote a pamphlet, now lost, on the occasion of the fall from power of one of Ireland's renowned politicians.
3. After graduating from college, Joyce began to write fiction.
4. At the time, Dublin was a city famous for its speakers, singers, and storytellers.
5. As a young boy, barely five, James stood up to his formidable Jesuit teachers, speaking and telling stories for himself and his classmates.
6. But it was not until he left Ireland to begin a famous exile that his gifts began to flower fully and he began to write *Dubliners*.
7. Before entering University College, Joyce had begun his writing career in earnest, and while there, he published an essay in a prestigious English journal.
8. In fact, all his mature work was written while he was in exile, and he died in Zurich, Switzerland, in 1941.

_____

_____

_____

_____

_____

_____

_____

II. *Begin with:* The farm is set in a small valley formed of gently rolling hills.

1. Once in the valley, you are surrounded by corn—two great yellow fields on either side of the road.
2. But when you arrive at the rise on which the house sits, you are surprised to see more of it than you had imagined was there.
3. One wing after another seems to jut out, willy-nilly.
4. A dirt road, covered over with thickets of birch and hawthorne brush, descends steeply and conducts your entrance into the valley via four-inch boards bridging a swift-flowing stream.
5. This road winds in a meander past hay fields, fodder silos, a cow barn, with the cows grazing sleepily behind it, on another small hill, and a kind of a lot containing some dozen pieces of farm machinery.
6. At this point, the farmhouse still looks small.
7. Even being close to all those wings gives you no real sense of its size.
8. You descend into the valley from a blacktop road built on a rise, sitting on one of those hills.
9. It's only when you are walking through the plain but pretty Nebraska-style rooms—and walk, and walk, and walk—that you actually realize the ampleness of this lovely farmhouse.

_____

_____

_____

_____

_____

_____

_____

_____

_____

_____

_____

_____

_____

_____

_____

III. *Begin with:* Law enforcement officials are agreed on what you should do if you find yourself being mugged.

1. Simply hand over whatever it is your assailant wants, money, jewelry, or your wallet.
2. Even a well-known karate expert concurs: "If someone pulled a gun on me and told me to hand over my wallet, I'd do it. A bullet travels faster than my foot."
3. The best defense against the mugger, police officers say, is to avoid isolated areas.
4. Nor must you attempt to use whatever weapons you have at hand; the mugger is likely to be too fast for you because the element of surprise is on his side.
5. First, do not resist.
6. But if you do feel a knife or a gun at your back, don't try to be a hero; give in and let your assailant leave as quickly as possible.
7. Moreover, you should hand it over carefully; do not make a sudden move or provocative gesture—the mugger may misunderstand and attack you without further ado.

8. Finally, obeying the first rule may be most important, for experts always recommend carrying a small amount of money to give a mugger; they say that much violence occurs when the mugger is frustrated by your having nothing for him to steal.
9. Don't pick up hitchhikers, and don't walk alone at night.
10. Next, do not attempt to negotiate with your man for some of your belongings; the delay could make him impatient and violent.
11. Another thing to avoid is the scream; if you are in an isolated area, it will not be heard, but if you are in a traveled area, the mugger may panic and start shooting or slashing.

B. The following paragraphs or parts of paragraphs need to be made into consistent wholes. Rewrite them, paying special attention to (1) logical order of sentences; (2) a consistent point of view; (3) shifts in person, tense, and number; and (4) transitional devices or other bridging techniques. Rewriting sentences to achieve coherence is permissible.

1. A hero is defined by those who use the word. I would have it apply to you if you risk your life or put your person in serious jeopardy to save another. You can exclude those who perform heroic deeds on behalf of a close relative. Somebody who rescues his mother or your child is so deeply motivated that the element of choice is removed; he can hardly do otherwise. What I need to have in my definition is this idea of disinterested action. The person who leaps to the rescue of a stranger—that's a hero.

2. Possessions are precious to us more for their associations than for their real monetary value. This rule seems to me to apply to the rich as well as a poor person, although certainly rich people cherish their expensive paintings, jewelry, and cars because of the money he paid for them. Associations with a thing lay in *how* we got them: A gift from a loved one made us value the sentiment associated with the person; an heirloom makes us proud of a heritage; a trophy gave us a sense of superior strength or skill; something you make with your own hands gives you value because people who make things realize a sense of accomplishment. You can only realize these sentiments from possessions associated with people, not with money.

3. To stop smoking, one must submit yourself to aversion therapy; it's the way that works best. It's based on the simple notion that we will have an aversion to anything that a person associates with pain or displeasure. The psychological theory is called behaviorism. When we are rewarded, we are reinforced in doing what brought you the reward; when you are punished, a person experiences the opposite. It sounds like fascism, but smoking is awful and we must give it up. The program involves a series of controlled experiences in which the smoker is made to associate their smoking habit with distasteful consequences. Eventually he or she is so averse to it that he gave it up.

4. Television makes zombies of those who watch it too much. The first step in the process took place when you found yourself flipping it on the minute you get home. When you start turning down opportunities to see friends because the person "just doesn't feel up to it," and then noticed that you "feel quite up to" . . . m*a*s*h, for example, you'll know you're in deep trouble. That person is withdrawing to zombieland. The trouble is now you're hooked and people don't care what you see, as long as your vision is turned to the tube and not elsewhere—life, for example. Television fare is sterile and takes us away from active pursuits. Everybody knows it except the zombie—and that could be you.

_____

_____

_____

_____

_____

_____

_____

_____

5. In the movie, *Raging Bull*, Robert DeNiro plays the prizefighter Jake Lamotta. He grew up in the Bronx in a tough neighborhood and is very tough; he was an animal, in fact. He took pleasure in fighting as hard as a person can fight, but he does not want to hook himself up to criminals in order to gain the championship. He got the championship on his own. He married a very beautiful neighborhood girl. He quarreled with his brother and accuses his wife of being unfaithful. Things go bad for him after his boxing career has ended and he went on to open a nightclub and become a kind of performing clown.

_____

_____

_____

_____

34 The Paragraph: Adequate Development

The third criterion for an effective paragraph is that it shall show adequate development. That is, we as readers wish to have an idea—the topic sentence—*fully* explained rather than only partly, teasingly, approached. For example, the following fragmentary groups of sentences are *not* adequately developed paragraphs:

1. Physical work can be a useful form of therapy for a mind in turmoil. Work concentrates your thoughts on a concrete task. Besides, it's more useful to work—you produce something rather than more anxiety or depression.

(The topic sentence seems like a good one. But what *is* a mind in turmoil? And, though it be true that work "concentrates thoughts," exactly *how* would such a discipline help the mind in turmoil? By failing to answer these questions, the fragment raises more questions than it answers.)

2. Professional athletes in America are poor role models for our youth. They tend to be self-centered and their other values are shallow. Besides, attaining major league status is more a matter of luck than anything else.

(This fragmentary paragraph fails because it fails to establish in any concrete way the exact nature of the professional athlete's life. In order to show the life not worthy of emulation, we must know what it *is*—concretely. Might it be a demanding pursuit of excellence, requiring years of self-sacrificing in the acquisition of physical skills? Might it also be that the professional athlete loses perspective in the glare of publicity and acquires meretricious values? Must he or she continually be hungry for money? Fame? Is he hounded to produce bigger and better performances? To what end? Why do they "tend to be self-centered?" Why are their "other values" shallow? And what are those "other values?")

3. Congressmen should be elected for longer terms. As it is, they must spend too much time in pursuit of reelection. A democracy needs experienced legislators.

(The last sentence suggests that most congressmen are replaced after two years and therefore cannot gain the necessary experience to do their jobs well. But this is only a suggestion. Moreover, we need more concrete details in support of the second sentence as well as an anticipatory rebuttal of the argument that too long a term in office would make a legislator unresponsive to public pressure.)

A. Take each fragmentary paragraph below and rewrite it so that its development is adequate. Of course, you will have to add concrete details, arguments, examples, reasons.

1. Freshmen at this college have a hard time when they first get here. After all, the sheer size of the place overwhelms. They've never seen anything like it.

_____

_____

_____

_____

_____

_____

_____

_____

_____

2. The crime rate is rising and something should be done about it. We need more police and a better criminal justice system. This would never happen in China.

_____

_____

_____

_____

_____

_____

_____

_____

_____

_____

3. Television crime shows give the world a distorted picture of an important aspect of American life. Not all crime is dealt with as *Kojak* deals with it. The whole thing is cockeyed.

_____

_____

_____

_____

_____

_____

_____

_____

4. People own pets for several very good reasons. I don't know any single people who *don't* have pets. If I were living alone, I'd get a scottie; they're the most affectionate breed of dog.

_____

_____

_____

_____

_____

_____

_____

_____

_____

_____

5. Foreign car manufacturers learned to develop economical small cars because they had to. In Japan, they import 95 percent of their petroleum. Germans are noted for their economical lifestyle.

_____

_____

_____

_____

_____

_____

_____

_____

B. For each topic sentence below, construct an adequately developed paragraph, using concrete details, reasons, or examples to illustrate or support it.

1. A student's first college registration can be a crushing experience.

_____

_____

2. One picture is not worth a thousand words.

3. A compact car has a number of advantages over a larger model.

_____

_____

_____

_____

_____

_____

4. Pro football appears to be America's favorite sport.

_____

_____

_____

_____

_____

_____

_____

_____

5. For short trips, air travel has no advantages over travel by car.

_____

_____

_____

_____

_____

_____

_____

_____

_____

_____

6. Keeping a diary can be a deflating experience.

_____

_____

_____

_____

_____

_____

_____

_____

7. Unlike fashions, mothers [or fathers, sisters, brothers, etc.] do not change from year to year [day to day, week to week, etc.].

_____

_____

_____

_____

_____

_____

_____

_____

_____

_____

8. Physical exercise can be dangerous [or vital] to your health.

_____

_____

_____

_____

_____

_____

_____

_____

9. Education and training are two different things.

_____

_____

_____

_____

_____

_____

_____

_____

_____

_____

10. Young children should be allowed to own pets.

_____

_____

_____

_____

_____

_____

_____

_____

_____

35   The Paragraph: Types of Development

It is easier to write fully developed paragraphs if the writer knows what job he has to do with the topic sentence. Specific types of topic sentences require specific types of development. Whatever type is finally employed, the paragraph should put concrete flesh onto the general idea controlling the paragraph: the topic sentence.

Most paragraphs can be developed by one of the following methods: *illustrative details, comparison and contrast, definition, classification, process analysis, causal analysis.*

Illustrative Details

This is the most common method of development and one of the most persuasive. All the other kinds have recourse to this method; it is hard to imagine a lively piece of writing that stays away from concrete details. The user of this method employs either a series of details, a few examples—each developed in a sentence or two—or a single striking example developed throughout the paragraph.

The thing most striking about working as a bank teller is the sense it gives you of how careless people are with their money. First, there are those who hurry up to you as if they were on fire and thrust a check for cashing under your nose. But when you give this type the money, they frequently walk away and just leave it in your tray. It's not uncommon for a customer to breathe a "thanks!" and then rush away without picking up a hundred dollars or even more. Then there are those who argue about their checking balances. Most often, these people have forgotten to deduct a check from their balances or added in a deposit they never made—hence, the discrepancy between what I say the balance is and what they think it is. More harsh words are spoken over this issue than any other. Finally, there are the careless check writers. These come in all shapes and sizes. The most common is the customer who writes one amount in figures and a different amount in words. But there are also a whole slew of them who forget to sign. It must be that they really can't part from their money very easily, which I suppose is a kind of wisdom and not careless at all.

(Notice that the writer uses three examples of people careless with their money and in so doing very nearly makes a classification.)

Comparison and Contrast

This is a common form of development in which two items are placed side by side to reveal similarities or differences. The method is useful in explaining one topic that is familiar by setting it alongside another that is not. For example, one can compare the British parliamentary system to our own congressional system, or Buddhism can be compared to Christianity for the same purpose. Another purpose is the argumentative one, which should be familiar to anyone who has ever weighed the virtues of two heads of lettuce, two apartments, two cars, and so on.

Both the Volkswagen and the Cadillac will get you where you want to go, but there the similarity ends. The Volks costs about $6,500 new, while the Cadillac will set you back more than twice that amount. The little jobbie costs 14 gallons of gas for every 500 miles she goes, but for the Caddie, going the same distance, you will pay for 25. If you break a fan belt on the smaller car, you will pay a modest price, but the Cadillac part is likely to cost you twice as much—as will other repairs; the car is that complicated compared to the import. You won't be able to park the Cadillac in a space under 8 feet; the Rabbit will squeeze into 5½. The big car will get you there more stylishly, but, as I said, both will get you where you want to go. And that's what counts.

(Notice that here the writer has chosen to compare the cars on the points of initial costs, gasoline cost, repair cost, and ease of parking. He might have chosen others, but the main point is that the cars are certainly comparable on these. Be sure not to compare items on points that can't stand comparison—a bird and a plane can be compared on aerodynamic efficiency but not on fuel consumption. Note, too, that the writer has chosen one of two possible structures. That is, he might also have spoken first about the Volkswagen and *all* the comparison points, and then have done the same for the Cadillac: first part about the Volkswagen, second about the Cadillac. Instead, he chose to talk about the two cars point by point.)

Definition

We are frequently called upon, in writing papers or in argumentative discussion, to define our terms. This is because most abstract matters admit of no full agreement on meaning. Ideas like *democracy* and *religion* change with changing times and need constant redefinition. The process of definition proceeds by relating the term to be defined to its generic class and then separating it from other members of the class through its differences from them.

Term to be defined	Genus (Class)	Differentia
Democracy	is a form of government	in which the people elect their governors.

The preceding we would call a formal definition. In paragraphs of definition, a writer may also employ details, examples, comparison and contrast, or other forms of development.

A dream is a series of images, ideas, and emotions that all of us experience in sleep. Although the phenomenon is universal, many deny that they dream. This is because an aspect of dream life is its absolute relevance to our deepest psychic life; those who deny that they dream are expressing their actual experience—they don't really remember their dreams—but are temporarily avoiding the content of these dreams. For the dream expresses, in symbolic form, the sleeper's most profound wishes, fears, and hopes. Most of these wishes are unacceptable to the dreamer in his conscious life; therefore, nature has provided the dream as a way of maintaining the vitality of this hidden life regardless of the conscious prohibitions. There are no easy "keys" to dreams. Each one is absolutely unique to the dreamer, and the way toward interpretation is hard: It involves the dreamer's "associating" words or ideas to elements of the dream until its significance comes clear—to the *dreamer*. A daydream, by contrast, is really a conscious phenomenon; the daydreaming person controls the content of the daydream, which is usually easily read as a symbolic enhancement of the daydreamer's ego.

(This definition begins with a formal one and then moves into examples of what is known about dreams—the causes, so to speak. The concluding sentences use comparison and contrast to make clear what the dream content really is.)

Classification

Classification groups together ideas or objects that have similarities. By doing this in a paragraph, the writer is able to explain and to develop a generalization. Classification is an ordinary way of thinking and functioning in the world; we see it every day, in the supermarket where items are grouped together (meat, dry cereal, produce, etc.) and in our homes where we use one room for one activity and a second for another.

Three kinds of nonworking eccentrics dominate my extended family. First, there were the Star-Struck. Cousin Shirley and Uncle Otto were members of this class. Shirley spent her time (until about age 50, as I recall) preparing herself for her big screen test. Most of her day she spent applying lotions, doing tummy-flattening exercises, and looking at *Modern Screen*. Work would "coarsen" her, she said. Otto, the trumpeter, couldn't work because he had to practice. So that was out for him, too. When Sousa came along and tapped them on the shoulder he'd make up for it. The second group, less sympathetic because less zany (though still eccentric), I'll call The Over-Qualified. This group was exemplified by Uncle Spencer. He was an astrophysicist before the term was invented and spent his time turning down the jobs my Aunt Ella went and dug up because he needed his time to polish a telescope lens that would cut through the Venusian clouds. No organization was up to his level of competence and vision. Aunt Ella went to work, eventually; Spencer went on polishing. The third group were the Invalids. My father was the prince of these. He had the diagnostic fervor of a first-year medical student and spent most of his life on long hiatuses and convalescences that gradually merged into one long career of nonemployment. Few members of my family fell outside these groups and I spent most of my formative years with them. How else would I have turned out to be a penniless writer?

175

(Here the classification has the effect of explaining the *cause* of the writer's condition, a humorous touch held back until the last sentence.)

Process Analysis

Any analysis is a taking apart; process analysis is a form of development which separates things into their separate parts to show either their structure or their function. It is a form most useful for explaining natural processes (metabolism or photosynthesis) or the functioning of a machine. It is also useful in giving directions (recipes or travel guides are process analyses) and frequently employs chronological or spatial order.

To study effectively for an examination, you need to establish a certain level of order in your methods. First, you cannot cram. Cramming only raises your anxiety level and anxiety is not conducive to mastery of material. Therefore, you need time. Begin your study at least three weeks before the exam date. Then divide the time and the material you need to master into matching, manageable units: so much on one day, so much on the next, and so forth. Manageable units would be special topics, such as intelligence (for a psychology course), acculturation (for a sociology course), chapters in texts, class notes, and so forth. Now you are ready to work. Read your materials carefully. Note with special attention the ideas and facts you have previously underscored. At the end of a study session, take the time to write out ideas and concepts in your own words until you have a good feel for them. Finally, ask a classmate to quiz you on what you have studied, and rearrange material into surprising combinations, as if to anticipate any surprising questions on the exam. Relax. If you have been orderly and conscientious you have nothing to worry about.

(Notice that the paragraph suggests an orderly process by using words to establish points of reference, that is, *first, next, now*, etc. Note, too, that there is a time order here.)

Causal Analysis

Where we wish to explain not a natural process or the functioning of a technical item but rather complex human affairs, we use the method of development called causal analysis. In this, we try to establish the series of causes behind some effect—say, the reasons why a particular American President was elected—or we try to establish the series of effects that will result from a particular cause—say the ways in which American domestic and foreign policy would change if a certain President were elected. It should be understood that given the complexity of human motive and event, no paragraph in causal analysis will be satisfying that ascribes a *single* cause to an event or predicts one effect from a single cause.

Criminologists and other experts see the recent increase in the crime rate as the result of a number of factors. For one thing, they say that the criminal justice system has broken down badly. Long delays in arraignments and trials have resulted in increased plea-bargaining. The result is that there is no longer a sense that justice is sure and swift—an idea that once worked as a deterrent. Moreover, some see the laws, part of the criminal justice system, to be at fault, for new laws mandate sentences of indeterminate length. This factor, they say, keeps first offenders in jail too long, giving them the opportunity to become repeated offenders by placing them in contact with "teachers," hardened criminals who teach them to be repeaters. Another factor is the improved system of crime reporting. More crime is being reported, in the category of rape, for example, sending the crime rate to higher levels. Finally, the whole complex of economic factors contributes. People on the lower fringes of the economic scale are more likely to slip over into criminal activity as economic indicators point to a squeeze on their life-style. Analysts have actually come up with statistical correlations to bolster this claim. And, in fact, there are even more causes of the increased crime rate, some of which we are just beginning to learn about.

(Several causes are adduced for the rise in the crime rate. Note that the writer relies on expert testimony about the causes, though he does not cite any specific data from a particular expert. Still, the paragraph is convincing because the logic of each cause cited seems strong.)

35 Exercise/THE PARAGRAPH: USING METHODS OF DEVELOPMENT

A. Which method would be most suitable for making a paragraph out of each of the following topic sentences? Give reasons. Then select two of these sentences and develop paragraphs using them.

1. The student union building here has very few suitable facilities compared to the one at my girl's college.

_____

_____

_____

_____

_____

_____

2. Burglary is on the increase for a number of reasons.

_____

_____

_____

_____

_____

_____

_____

3. Getting ready to write a composition for this course is really an ordeal.

_____

_____

_____

_____

_____

_____

_____

_____

_____

4. Intelligence is the capacity to face what you do not know how to do.

_____

_____

_____

_____

_____

_____

_____

_____

5. Religion is based on a belief in the afterlife.

_____

_____

_____

_____

_____

_____

_____

_____

_____

6. There are three kinds of male students on this campus.

_____

_____

_____

_____

_____

_____

_____

_____

_____

7. I never felt so sick as I did after my last math exam.

_____

_____

_____

_____

_____

_____

_____

8. Making maple syrup is a long, slow process.

9. The human respiratory system is connected to other vital organ systems.

_____

_____

10. The three kinds of exam givers on this campus are all represented in my courses this term.

_____

_____

_____

_____

_____

_____

_____

_____

B. *My attitudes toward being a working student have changed since I came to college.*

Using this topic sentence, write three separate paragraphs. In the first, explain *why* this change has taken place. In the second, explain *how* these attitudes have changed. In the third, compare and contrast the two sets of attitudes, that is, the ones you had before you came to college and the ones you have now.

1. _____

_____

_____

_____

_____

_____

2. _____

_____

_____

_____

_____

_____

_____

_____

_____

3. _____

_____

_____

_____

_____

_____

_____

_____

_____

36   The Thesis Statement

The *thesis statement* of an essay is its central idea written out as a sentence. Ideally, the thesis statement arises out of the thinking you do when generating materials for an essay. When you think you are ready to write out your thesis statement, test it against the following criteria of effectiveness.

1. An effective thesis statement is limited or narrowed down from a larger statement or from a set of materials you have gathered for your essay. The idea in doing this is to make sure that you have a limited and thus manageable territory to cover.

Statement Too Large   Our city's transportation system is a poor one.
Manageably Limited   Our city's bus schedules are inconvenient for both workers and shoppers.

Statement Too Large   Colleges don't have adequate advisement services for their students.
Manageably Limited   State College has inadequate advisement services for engineering majors.

2. An effective thesis statement is singular: It ordinarily has no compound parts.

Multiple   Inflation is fueled by too much available consumer credit, oil prices that are too high, and too steep a rise in the prices of basic consumer goods.
Singular   Inflation is fueled by too much available consumer credit.
Inflation is fueled by oil prices that are too high.
Inflation is fueled by too steep a rise in the prices of basic consumer goods.

Multiple   An engineering student's basic needs are to know mathematics, to understand mechanics, and to have a good idea of the limits of his field.
Singular   An engineering student's most basic need is to have a good grasp of mathematics.
An engineering student's most important need is an understanding of mechanics.
An engineering student's primary need is to begin with a good idea of the limits of his field.

3. An effective thesis statement is concrete.

Vague   Reggae music is interesting because of its content.
Concrete   Reggae music is interesting because its content makes statements about the black heritage.

Vague   My biology class is interesting.
Concrete   My biology class provokes exciting discussions on the exact nature of
living matter.

---

36   Exercise/RECOGNIZING AND MAKING EFFECTIVE THESIS STATEMENTS

A. Using the criteria just discussed, examine each of the thesis statements
printed below. Which are effective? Which not? Why?

1. Magazine advertising is confusing.

_____

_____

_____

_____

2. Living in dormitories has the advantages of being close to campus facilities,
providing an opportunity for social life, and costing less than off-campus
housing.

_____

_____

_____

_____

3. Inflation is caused by an upward spiral of prices and wages, and its effects
on students are devastating.

_____

_____

_____

4. The safety of an American President cannot be guaranteed by the Secret Service.

_____

_____

_____

_____

_____

5. People's tendency to have bad manners is most evident in a crowded sports arena.

_____

_____

_____

_____

_____

6. Intercollegiate baseball costs more money than it's worth.

_____

_____

_____

_____

7. The town I grew up in provided too few opportunities for a young woman to socialize.

_____

_____

_____

_____

_____

8. My difficulties in physics lab are tremendous.

_____

_____

_____

_____

_____

9. The new engineering curriculum restricts a student's choices and places too much emphasis on mathematics.

_____

_____

_____

_____

_____

10. A person's hobby is the key to that person's character.

_____

_____

_____

_____

_____

B. Using the following broad subjects, construct for each an effective thesis statement for a brief composition.

1. (television violence)

   _____

   _____

2. (high school teachers and college teachers)

   _____

   _____

3. (summer jobs)

   _____

   _____

4. (sports cars)

   _____

   _____

5. (dating on this campus)

   _____

   _____

6. (snowmobiles)

   _____

   _____

7. (the costs of higher education)

   _____

   _____

8. (religion in American life)

_____

_____

9. (rural life and city life)

_____

_____

10. (teacher attitudes on this campus)

_____

37　Planning: The Outline

An important stage in planning the essay is writing an outline. The outline divides your material into manageable units and describes the order in which you will present them. By the use of several levels of ranking, the outline also suggests the relative importance of these units.

The two types of outline important in your college work are the *sentence outline* and the *topic outline*. The advantage of the sentence outline is that each entry must be a complete sentence; this requirement forces the writer to think more clearly about his materials, but the sentence outline takes longer to write than the topic outline. On the other hand, the topic outline takes less of the writer's time, but because it uses only phrases, usually a noun and a modifier, the writer may not feel as securely in control with it as with a sentence outline.

Whichever type you use, be sure that your outline is soundly constructed by testing it against these criteria of effectiveness.

1. Use conventional notation and logical form:

I. . . . .

  A. . . . .

    1. . . . .

      a. . . . .

      b. . . . .

    2. . . . .

  B. . . . .

II. . . . . , and so on

The meaning of this notation is that the part labeled roman numeral I has been divided into two parts, A and B. A has been further divided into 1 and 2. The part designated 1 has been further divided into a and b. Thus the principle should be clear: You cannot divide your essay into fewer than two parts (I and II in the example) and cannot divide any heading into fewer than two parts—though you need *not* divide one if it seems indivisible to you. Thus every essay must have at least a I and a II. Every time your I has an A, moreover, it must also have a B; if your A has a 1, it must have a 2, and so forth. Remember: Everything is connected; each subhead should be related to the heading above it.

2. Be sure that your outline covers your subject adequately. The major headings in your outline (those given roman numerals) should include enought material to satisfy the expectations provoked by your subject.

THE TERRORS OF REGISTRATION

Inadequate Material	*Adequate Material*
I. Inexperienced freshman	I. Inexperienced freshman
II. Difficulties of choices	II. Difficulties of choices
III. Attitudes of registration officers	III. Attitudes of registration officers
	IV. Crush of people
	V. Lack of physical amenities
	VI. Lack of help from upperclassmen
	VII. Closed courses

The reader would obviously expect the material on the right and be disappointed with the skimpiness of the material on the left. Be sure that your outline is exposed to this criterion so that you can avoid such disappointments.

3. Be sure that your major headings follow some logical order. Some consistent principle must govern the progression of your major headings. Chronology is one such principle, cause and effect another. There are others. The point is to be consistent and use only one of these.

Consistent Time Order	*Mixed Order*
ARRANGING A DINNER PARTY	CRIME
I. Selecting the date	I. Its increase since 1975 (time order)
II. Inviting the guests	II. Its causes (cause and effect order)
III. Preparing the menu	III. Robbery versus rape (order by classification)
IV. Cooking the food	
V. Setting the table	
VI. The service	

If your outline fails to meet this criterion, you are probably uncertain of your whole approach and need to reexamine your central idea or thesis statement.

4. Be sure to cast groups of headings and subheadings in parallel grammatical form. Examine the two outlines below. Both were prepared for a paper entitled "The Energy Crisis in Oil and Two Alternate Sources of Power."

Topic Outline

I. The Arab oil embargo of 1973
  A. Shortage of oil
  B. Dwindling of resources

II. Alternative source: nuclear power
  A. Expensive
  B. Dangerous
  C. Limited

III. Alternative source: solar power
  A. Inexpensive
  B. Safe
  C. Limitless
  D. Needing technology

Sentence Outline

I. The Arab oil embargo of 1973 pointed up the need for America to find alternate sources of fuel.
  A. The embargo produced a shortage of fuel.
  B. The embargo reminded us that all our fossil fuel resources are limited.

II. Nuclear power as an alternative, though widely favored, is not likely to be the answer.
  A. It's very expensive—both for new plant construction and for fuel processing.
  B. It's very dangerous.
  C. It's also likely to prove a limited resource.

III. Solar power, though not widely favored, is probably a more attractive alternative.
  A. It's relatively inexpensive except for start-up costs.
  B. It's easy to handle and not dangerous.
  C. The supply is limitless.
  D. It's likely to require a new technology.

Notice that in the topic outline IA and IB are parallel (noun phrases) as are IIA, IIB, IIC (adjectives). In the sentence outline, IA and IB are parallel, but they are not parallel with IIA, IIB, IIC—which are parallel with one another.

Note: The parallelism rule applies to *groups of headings;* the whole outline need not be parallel. This criterion is important because parallel form assures that you treat ideas in a similar manner, thus making it easy for a reader to follow your argument and giving coherence and logic to your presentation.

192

37 Exercise/MASTERING THE OUTLINE FORM

A. Below is a portion of a sentence outline for a paper entitled "Student Deficiencies and How to Correct Them." Study it carefully and criticize it according to the criteria we have just discussed.

II. To improve your reading skills, you need three things.
    A. Motive
        1. You should need to do so.
    B. You must have good study discipline.
        1. You should be able to undertake regular reading sessions over a substantial period of time.
        2. It also requires patience to endure slow progress.
    C. You must have a good dictionary and use its resources.
        1. The dictionary helps improve your comprehension.
        2. Using new words by writing many sentences to assure you really have them in your head.

_____

_____

_____

_____

_____

_____

_____

_____

B. Below is a portion of a sentence outline for a paper called "Managing Student Finances." As you can see, certain entries are blank. Develop this portion of the outline by filling in the blanks appropriately.

III. A student sorely in need of money has two choices.
    A. You may go to work.
        1. _____

2. _____

B. You may try to borrow money.

   1. _____

   2. _____

   3. If the money cannot be borrowed, the student can profit in two ways.

     a. _____

     b. _____

  C. Test the following major headings according to criterion number 3 (logical order, p. 191).

HOW TO BUY A CAR

  I. Registration and insurance

 II. Checking the engine and other mechanical parts

III. The reliability of the dealer and/or other seller

IV. Deciding what you want and can afford

  V. Sources of good used cars

  D. "How to Achieve Success in College Life" is the title of an essay for which is given below an outline with a number of headings missing. Fill them in.

  I. A student's expectations must be realistic.
    A. You must be prepared for work—not a picnic.
    B. You cannot be surprised at how small you are in the context of the college's size.

     1. _____

     2. _____

 II. You must develop a certain level of maturity.
    A. This will help you in planning your program wisely.
    B. It will also assist you in getting close to professors who can help you.

III. You should bring with you or develop fairly quickly good, disciplined work habits.

    A. _____

    B. _____

    C. _____

1. _____

2. _____

IV. You should have the ability to get along with others.

A. _____

B. _____

E. Take any one of the topics suggested in Section 35 and work it up into a three-level sentence outline.

38　Introductions for the Essay

The introduction is the first basic part of your essay. (The others are the *main body* and the *conclusion*.) The importance of the introduction cannot be overstressed. It presents the reader with your first words; therefore, it is your first contact with the reader and it can either make or break your relationship with that reader. It need not be very long; four of five sentences will do for a five-hundred word essay. But it must (1) capture the reader's attention, (2) identify and set some sort of limit on your subject (in this portion of the essay, you could make your thesis statement), and (3) establish the tone of the writing—that is, tell the reader how you will *treat* your subject. Here is a list of things to bear in mind when thinking about how to write your introduction:

1. You may use an anecdote—a piece of personal experience that is striking.
2. You can make an unusual statement—one that you know will catch the reader's attention because it goes against the grain of conventional wisdom, for example, "Most of our distinguished economists think the American economy is in trouble—they're wrong."
3. You might consider stating and illustrating your thesis at once.
4. Briefly give the reader the background of the subject by way of justifying (stating the need for) your essay.
5. Open with a challenge to the reader, for example, "If you want your marriage to continue to be a routine and ultimately deadening experience, read no further."
6. *Do not* begin with material not relevant to your subject.
7. *Do not* say things like "I intend to write an essay on the topic of _____ ." Write the introduction to that essay; the reader knows your intention: The essay is evidence of it.
8. *Do not* fail to write an introduction that gives some sense of your subject; in other words, don't plunge in by covering at once your main points.

38 Exercise/RECOGNIZING AND CONSTRUCTING EFFECTIVE INTRODUCTIONS

A. Examine the following introductions. Which do you consider effective? Why? Which ineffective? Why? How could you make a better one for the given topic?

1. Registration for Freshmen: A Nerve-Shattering Experience

If you think cruelty to freshmen at this college is a normal part of their education, read no further. If, however, you wonder about the effects of registration on a perfectly innocent newcomer, the following may interest you. It illustrates the human cost of administrative "efficiency."

2. Dating at State College: What It Feels Like to Be in a Fishbowl

Animals are the proper subject for study, not people. The trouble with dating at this college is that there are so few places to go with your date that a couple invariably find themselves among classmates. These people are only human, and pretty soon they're looking at you—intensely. Being under scrutiny like that, the daters never get a chance to enjoy the date.

_____

_____

_____

_____

_____

_____

3. Woodworking Is Not as Difficult as It Sounds

Don't let the professionals get to you. Woodworking is pretty easy if you'll just stay cool. I remember people telling me I couldn't ski and two weeks later I was working really difficult trails. I intend to write an essay on the subject of how easy it is to do woodworking and enjoy it.

_____

_____

_____

_____

_____

_____

_____

_____

4. The United Nations Should Be Abolished

The United Nations is a farce. It never stops wars. Think of all the wars we've had since it was founded: Korea, Middle East, Vietnam, etc. Besides, it gives people a false sense of security. It's also very expensive to maintain and gives the newly developing nations a false sense of cooperation so that they put their hopes in the U.N. instead of working hard in their own interests by themselves.

_____

_____

_____

_____

_____

_____

_____

_____

5. The Effects of Modern Technology on Our Ecosystems

Modern technology is quite amazing. In the last century, we have seen the rise of automated industries, chemical innovations, communications, space travel, and instant, worldwide television. All these have had effects on the quality of our environment. Everybody knows it. It's obvious everywhere you turn. Just notice the noise and dirt in your own local environment and you'll have a beginning idea of what it's all about.

_____

_____

_____

_____

_____

_____

_____

_____

B. For each title given below, write an effective introduction, bearing in mind the list of hints given in the text of this section.

1. How to Make Excellent Prints in Your Own Darkroom

_____

_____

_____

_____

_____

_____

_____

2. Women's Fashions in the 1980s

_____

_____

_____

_____

_____

_____

_____

_____

_____

3. The Value of Space Travel

_____

_____

_____

_____

_____

_____

_____

_____

4. Keeping Your Small Car Running

_____

_____

_____

_____

_____

_____

_____

_____

_____

_____

5. Required Courses at This College

_____

_____

_____

_____

_____

_____

_____

6. The Lure of an Oceanside Vacation

_____

_____

_____

_____

_____

39   Conclusions for the Essay

Most frustrating to a sensitive reader is a piece of writing that simply trails off into a meaningless generalization or one that ends abruptly. When a reader has finished your conclusion, he needs to have the sense that he has just had a rounded-off experience—that something has been satisfactorily *finished*.

The techniques for achieving this effect in your conclusion are the following:

1. Conclude with a restatement of your thesis statement or main idea, preferably in some varied form—that is, using different but equally clear and effective words.
2. Conclude with a very brief summary of your main points, thus reminding the reader of the effective things you've just been saying.
3. Conclude with some form of 1 or 2 but then add a climactic point—something new and effective to seal and certify what you've been saying all along.
4. Use a short anecdote or personal experience that will illustrate the truth and relevance of what you've been saying.

If your conclusion follows methods 1 through 3, the reader's satisfaction will be gained from having read your materials twice, that is, once in the beginning and once at the end. If you use method 4, this satisfaction will result from a movement from the general to the particular.

---

39   Exercise/CONSTRUCTING EFFECTIVE CONCLUSIONS

For each of the four topics provided below, write four conclusions, one employing each method discussed. Before you begin, you must write a thesis statement for each.

Example   The Advantages of Owning a Small Car

Thesis Statement There are three distinct advantages to owning a small car: economy, ease of repair, and convenience in handling.

CONCLUSIONS USING VARIOUS TECHNIQUES

Method 1 (variation on thesis statement)

The money you will save by owning a small car might actually buy you a smaller one; the few headaches you get from repair problems will enable you to live a carefree life; and the convenience of the little bug will make you seem to your friends a masterly manipulator of the things of this world.

Method 2 (brief summary of main points)

The savings on initial price, insurance, and gas are astonishing. The simplicity of the machine assures that parts and labor will be quickly there when you need them. And the way you are able to maneuver, change gears, shift speeds, park anyplace you wish—these are nothing but enviable.

Method 3 (some restatement plus a climactic point)

Not only will this kind of car spare you money, wear and tear on your psyche, and the difficulties of wrestling with a big brute of a gas guzzler, but owning a small car will make you special. It will give you the sense that in this world of ever bigger things and ever bigger problems, you are modestly going about your business, contributing to a world less greedy and less expansive.

Method 4 (ending with an anecdote or personal experience)

Last week, during the big snowstorm, a car skidded down the street where my car and several others were parked, bouncing off mine and my neighbor's much bigger machine with about equal force. After both of us inspected our damaged vehicles, I grabbed the big dent in my right front fender and manhandled it back into place. Then I drove to school. My neighbor went dejectedly back into his house and phoned for the wrecker. Moral: If you want to do it alone, elect the small one.

Living in an Apartment Off-Campus

Thesis Statement

_____

_____

_____

Method 1

_____

_____

_____

Method 2

Method 3

_____

_____

_____

_____

Method 4

_____

_____

_____

_____

_____

_____

_____

_____

_____

Preparing for a Career in Business (or Law, Medicine, Engineering)

Thesis Statement

_____

_____

_____

Method 1

_____

_____

_____

_____

_____

_____

_____

_____

_____

Method 2

_____

_____

_____

_____

_____

_____

_____

_____

_____

Method 3

_____

_____

_____

_____

_____

_____

_____

_____

_____

Method 4

_____

_____

_____

_____

_____

_____

_____

_____

_____

The Dangers of Nuclear Energy

Thesis Statement

_____

_____

_____

Method 1

_____

_____

_____

_____

_____

_____

_____

Method 2

_____

_____

_____

_____

_____

_____

_____

_____

Method 3

_____

_____

_____

_____

_____

_____

_____

_____

Method 4

_____

_____

_____

_____

_____

_____

_____

Prolife versus Prochoice: Is There a Clear Answer?

Thesis Statement

_____

_____

_____

Method 1

_____

_____

_____

_____

_____

_____

_____

_____

Method 2

_____

_____

_____

_____

_____

_____

_____

_____

Method 3

_____

_____

_____

_____

_____

_____

_____

Method 4

_____

_____

_____

_____

_____

_____

_____

_____

_____

If you have made an effective outline from a carefully and thoughtfully constructed thesis statement, you are now ready for the fun part—the actual writing of the composition. Because of your careful planning, things should go smoothly because much of your anxiety is gone: you *know* what to write and in what order. You *know* how to begin and how to end your essay.

Take your time now and write out your essay.

_____

_____

_____

_____

_____

_____

_____

_____

_____

_____

_____

_____

_____

40A Rewriting the Essay

All writers rewrite. Very good writers rewrite a great deal in order to improve on their first or subsequent drafts. If you have planned properly for your first draft, then *rewriting to a second or third can never do anything but improve your essay.*

Now, using the following checklist, examine and then rewrite the parts of the composition that need the work.

1. Is your introduction effective? Is it likely to catch the reader's attention? Have you mentioned your subject? Limited it? Or does it ramble away from the topic?
2. Examine each main point. Is it fully developed? Can you think of a better concrete detail in illustration or support of your topic sentence?
3. Does each paragraph really relate to your central idea?
4. Look specifically at each sentence to be sure that each word means what you intend it to mean. Can you replace some words with more accurate ones? Phrases? Clauses?
5. Is your style interesting, with sentences of varied length, or is it breathy with very long sentences? Is it filled with short, choppy little sentences? Repair the style where it needs repairing.
6. Does each paragraph flow coherently (with a smooth bridge) into the next?
7. Examine your conclusion. Does it give readers the sense of completeness and wholeness that they must have to be satisfied with what you've written? Make effective repairs.

_____

_____

_____

_____

_____

41 Proofreading: The Final Touches

Disciplined writers are motivated by the wish to communicate clearly and the pride of craftsmanship to deliver their work in as perfect a state as they can attain. That means that proofreading—*after rewriting*—as a final step is essential.

To proofread is to painstakingly go over each letter of each word of what you've written—using a pen or pencil pointing at the letters as it moves across the page. Very experienced writers can sometimes do their proofreading by keeping in mind all the things they must look for; so they only proofread once or twice. Less experienced writers should use a checklist until such time as they are able to do without one.

Now proofread your last draft, using the checklist that follows. Proofread your essay *once for each item on the list.*

1. Is the paper legible? Can a reader *read* what you've written without having to strain to *decode* it? Typewritten papers may have to be retyped and handwritten ones recopied if the paper is a mass of scratches and ink marks. Consult your instructor on the level of legibility and neatness he or she requires.
2. Did you, in the heat of composition, omit necessary words? Restore them.
3. Are the grammar and punctuation correct? A run-on sentence, a subject-verb agreement error, a faulty sequence of tenses, a misplaced comma—one or more of these errors can affect the reader's confidence in you. (That is, if you cannot be trusted with the small things—grammar and punctuation—how can you be trusted with the big ones—the ideas you're discussing?)
4. Are all the words spelled correctly?
5. Are there habitual errors here, ones that you make frequently? Correct them.
6. It's still not too late to *rewrite* (see the checklist in Section 40A).

Mechanics

42   Capitalization

Capital letters are used in the following ways.

At the beginning of a sentence:

The rose is a fragrant flower.

For the pronoun I and the interjection O:

My father and I never said O.

For days of the week, months, holidays:

We leave Friday for the whole month of March and will be back by Easter.

For titles of books, plays, movies, TV shows, short stories, and poems, the first letters of main words only:

We won't watch Archie Bunker's Place this week; instead, we'll read aloud from Dickens's Bleak House.

For proper names, adjectives, and official titles:

There will be a speech by the Reverend Kathy Rose, a Christian orator.

For historical events, terms, and artifacts:

The Declaration of Independence was written during the French Revolution, both of which were products of the Enlightenment.

For special terms associated with universities and colleges:

The Dean advised me to take Biology 135.

For the names of public and private buildings:

We're having lunch at the World Trade Center.

For the names of both public and private organizations:

The U. S. Department of Agriculture has good relations with the Iowa Farmers' Grain Cooperative.

For virtually all references to things religious; deities, churches, or adjectives based on these:

According to the Mosaic law, murder is a crime, to which Allah would agree.

For products referred to by brand name:

I'm using Kleenex to wipe the screen of my Sony before I eat my Wheaties.

Read carefully each of the following sentences. Where there is an error in capitalization, correct it. If the sentence is correct as it stands, write *C* in the space provided.

1. _____ Frank's mother was Irish, his father was Columbian, and he was raised as a catholic.

2. _____ The Professor who taught English 202 changed my entire attitude toward Modern Literature.

3. _____ When Marge saw *Petrified Forest*, she fell madly in love with Leslie Howard.

4. _____ Tuesday, November 4, is election day; honor your voting privilege as an american.

5. _____ For some reason, my Aunt always gets depressed in february.

6. _____ Swedish tennis pro Bjorn Borg, who won the Wimbledon title this year, lost the U. S. Open Championship at flushing meadow stadium in new york.

7. _____ We won't be able to afford a xerox machine for our office until the Spring.

8. _____ On the fourth of july, we all went to see the James Bond movie, *Moonraker*.

9. _____ Simon Marsden is a photographer whose work is part of the permanent collection of the Albert and Victoria Museum in London.

10. _____ When Donna was at Harvard, I used to take the amtrak train to Boston every friday to visit her.

11. _____ I went to the High School of Performing Arts in New York, and it was very different from the way it was depicted in the movie *Fame*.

12. _____ My brother stole a Sony color television set and i don't know if i should call The Police.

13. _____ Paula gave me the *Oxford English Dictionary* for christmas, but it's such a cumbersome volume that I usually refer to the smaller *Webster's New International Dictionary*.

14. _____ A Turkish person might resent being referred to as an Arab, but I don't really understand the distinction.

15. _____ She bought a fresh bluefish at the fulton street fish market, and it came wrapped in a page from yesterday's Portland *Oregonian*.

16. _____ The convention center in Atlanta is a marvel of modern Architecture.

17. _____ You don't know how beautiful America really is until you've traveled in the midwest.

18. _____ The dean has removed *portnoy's complaint,* by Philip Roth, from all english department reading lists.

19. _____ waitresses at the Wild Bunch Wine Bar make a fortune in tips on Fridays and Saturdays.

20. _____ Pierre lent me his chewed-up copy of *The Confessions of Felix Krull,* and it completely fell apart before I could finish it.

43 Italics

Italics is the name given to the typeface in which these words are written. Italics are indicated in handwritten or typewritten manuscripts by underlining the words to be italicized. Use italics for the names of books, plays, movies, television shows, newspapers, magazines, ships, aircraft, musical compositions, foreign words and phrases that have not become part of the English language, words and phrases considered for themselves, scientific words in Latin, or to give special emphasis to an ordinary word or words in a sentence.

The Executioner's Song by Norman Mailer
Shakespeare's _Hamlet_
The Empire Strikes Back
Three's Company
The Washington _Post_ (note that the name of the city is not italicized)
The Washington Monthly
Queen Elizabeth II (ship)
The Spirit of St. Louis (aircraft)
Mozart's _40th Symphony_
pied-à-terre; raison d'être; bon vivant
The term _bottom line_ is often used by business people.
The fish commonly called the loach is a species of _Colbitis_ or _Nemachilus_.
What's important is not what he _said_ but what he _did_.

---

43 Exercise/THE PROPER USE OF ITALICS

A. Write sentences as indicated and use the italics required.

1. (a sentence naming a book title)

_____

_____

2. (a sentence using the name of a newspaper)

_____

_____

3. (a sentence using a foreign word or phrase)

_____

_____

4. (a sentence naming a magazine)

_____

_____

5. (a sentence using the title of a television show)

_____

_____

B. Some of the following sentences show the correct use of italics. Next to these write *C.* Some sentences, however, need to have italics removed or added. In these, make the appropriate additions or deletions.

1. _____ In the same week, Bruce Springsteen was featured on the covers of both Time and Newsweek.

_____

_____

2. _____ He calls it a strombis pugilis; I call it a pretty shell.

_____

_____

3. _____ All the forms must be filled out in *triplicate.*

_____

_____

4. _____ The program included Antonio Vivaldi's *Il Favorito.*

_____

_____

5. _____ I didn't think the remake of King Kong was nearly as good as the original.

_____

_____

6. _____ I couldn't describe what Jim does for a living except to say that he's an *entrepreneur.*

_____

_____

7. _____ My friend Nina, who grew up in England, drops her final r's.

_____

_____

8. _____ The fin-de-siècle fashions have inspired Halston's new fall line.

_____

_____

9. _____ I always have trouble pronouncing the word schism.

_____

_____

10. _____ The new synthetic furs *look* like the real thing, but they don't *feel* the same.

_____

_____

11. _____ I read recently that the television show Sesame Street may be over-stimulating for children, and ultimately detract from their ability to concentrate on one thing for any length of time.

_____

_____

12. _____ The Orient Express, no longer in existence, used to run from Paris all the way to Beirut.

_____

_____

44   Abbreviations

Although abbreviations can save a writer time and space, not all abbreviations are acceptable in essay writing. Convention governs which may and which may not be used.

Appropriate

Forms of address and titles: Mr., Mrs., Ms., Messrs., Mmes., St., Jr., Sr., M.D., D.D.S., A.B. (or B.A.), M.A., Ph.D., and Esq. (for Esquire, a title used only by lawyers).

Certain useful foreign words and phrases: c. or ca. (about), cf. (compare), e.g. (for example), i.e. (that is), v. (see), viz. (namely).

Technical terms: BTU (British Thermal Unit), cc or cm^3 (cubic centimeter), cm (centimeter), gm (gram), km (kilometer), kmh (kilometers per hour), mpg (miles per gallon), mph (miles per hour), rpm (revolutions per minute).

Organizations, institutions, government agencies, trade unions (when these form pronounceable words they are called *acronyms*): UNESCO, FBI, CBS, VISTA, AFL–CIO.

Expressions of time: 1453 B.C. (before Christ); A.D. 973 (Anno domini; in the year of our Lord); 8 a.m. or A.M., p.m. or P.M.; EST (Eastern Standard Time); DST, MST, CST, PST.

Inappropriate

Do not abbreivate the following in a written text, though some may be useful in addresses or certain short references.

Titles: Not *Prof.* but *Professor* Dennis Turner. Not *Sen.* but *Senator* Jacqueline Jaffe.

Given names: Not *Geo.*, *Wm.*, *Thos.*, *Ed.*, *Jas.*, *Theo.*, but *George*, *William*, *Thomas*, *Edward*, *James*, *Theodore*.

Days of the week, names of months or holidays: Not The king dies on *Tues.*, but *Tuesday*. Not I'm planning a vacation in *Aug.*, but *August*. Not for *Xmas*, I'd like a camera, but for *Christmas*.

Places: Not I live in *M.M.,* but *New Mexico.* Not Take County *Rd.,* but *Road* to Sarah's house.

Units of measurement: Not *ins., ft., yds., mi., lbs., oz.,* but *inches, feet, yards, miles, pounds, ounces.*

Academic courses: Not I am taking *eco.* and *psych.* this term. Better to take *economics* and *psychology.*

Ampersand (&): Don't use it in place of *and* unless it is part of an official company name, for instance, *Arthur Zeiger & Daughter, Inc.*

Ordinary words: Not *thru* for *through, mtns.* for *mountains, tho* for *though, yrs* for *yours,* or the like.

---

44 Exercise/USING ABBREVIATIONS CORRECTLY

Each sentence below contains errors in the use of abbreviations. Correct each one.

1. Doctor Waldhorn took the stand and testified that at 8 am, when the murder took place, he was smoking & drinking.

2. The trouble with Kan. is that it's too flat.

3. I'm thru with Xmas; from now on I'm spending my holiday in Fla.

4. When she began to gain weight, she was 202 lbs, 12 oz, but after awhile she weighed even more.

5. They fought like cats every Mon., Wed., and Fri.

6. Mine is the one on the right, yrs. is the one on the left.

7. I'd like to travel down to the tip of S.A.

8. The mtns. in Penna. are neat, better than those in W.Va.

9. I'm failing eco. and psych. this term.

10. The Committee on Urban Betterment announced a new program to train city mothers for better employment opportunities. A spokesman said "CUB embraces mothers, mine, yrs., everybody's."

11. Sen. Mintz and Sen. Gray announced a new program to aid drs. in distress.

12. The Gov. told the Pres. that Malcolm Bosse, Junior, would be an acceptable candidate for the new judgeship.

45   Numerals

Consistency is the first rule to be observed here. Either use numerals or spell out the numbers in words. Don't mix the two, unless there is a special reason for doing so (see below, number 4). There are conventional rules governing the use of numerals:

1. Spell out numbers that require no more than two words. In other cases, use numerals.

There were *seventy-five* cases of flu in our area last week.
My federal tax refund came to $88.37.

2. In writing dates, addresses, percentages followed by the symbol %, page numbers, or the time of day followed by a.m. or p.m., use numerals.

3. Use numerals for quantities in scientific or technical writing.

4. It is appropriate to use in the same sentence a combination of words and numerals where such a combination is necessary for clarity.

You may take only six 6-inch trout from this stream.

5. Do not begin a sentence with a numeral that is not spelled out.

6. If your text contains a great many numbers or a mixture of whole numbers and decimals, it is preferable to use numerals for all of them.

---

45   Exercise/USING NUMERALS CORRECTLY

Each of the sentences given has an error in the handling of numerals. Correct each.

1. 2,000 years ago, 13 people attended an extraordinary last meal.

2. It was a reading of seventy-seven point seven that alerted us to the thirteen point five pounds of pressure; in eighteen hundred cubic centimeters of nitrogen, we dissolved four hundred eighty two point nine grams of liquid sodium and tried to relieve the pressure that way.

3. I promised to pay the government ninety four hundred seventy five dollars every year until my debt to them was discharged.

4. The father is 54, the mother is 37, and the children are 3 and 1.

5. His author's royalties amounted to twelve and a half percent of sales.

6. 9 years ago, I was just a little boy of 3.

7. Including taxes, the price came to six thousand seven hundred and forty dollars and 88 cents.

8. On October nineteenth, nineteen twenty-six, he came home to find he had a new baby brother; the boy looked a hundred and thirty four years old.

9. My office number is nine thirty eight and I'm usually there until six p.m.

10. On page twelve, he manages to introduce the hero—finally.

11. Uncle Bud won the marathon with a time of two hours, six and a half minutes flat.

12. The circumference was thirty-seven hundred and thirty-seven one-hundredths inches.

13. She spent $.85 for lunch.

14. Physics one twenty five will be given on Tuesday afternoons.

15. 6 of my uncles gathered for my mother's birthday.

46   Exercise/MECHANICS REVIEW TEST

Proofread the following paragraphs for errors in capitalization, italics, abbreviation, and the use of numerals.

1. In canada, there are at least fifteen thousand five hundred and fifty rivers and lakes. Each of these is teeming with fish and many books, the most famous of which is Fishing Canadian Waters by J. walton, describe the pleasures of angling in the waters of our Northern Neighbor. All year round, Canada's waters abound in Pike, walleye, Salmon, perch, and muskelunge. Trout streams in Ontario and Manitoba only require a slight stirring of the surface to lure to the surface dozens of the speckled beauties Salvelina and Salmo. In Mordecai Richler's novel, Duddy Kravitz, the canadian jewish hero makes a fetish of catching P. flavescens, commonly known as the perch. Most Canadians who fish do not fail to visit the maritime provinces for the best angling in that great country.

2. Alan Alda, best known as the star of the cbs tv series m*a*s*h, is also well-known as a director and an actor in the film medium. The author of the seduction of joe tynan also starred in that film with meryl streep; later, he directed the four seasons. Earlier, he had a considerable acting career in such famous works as the apple tree, a letter to my mother, and the candy man.

3. It is not uncommon for a 5'10" basketball player to thrill a crowd used to seeing taller athletes. 19,000 fans will leap to their feet to see the relatively small Calvin Murphy or the somewhat taller Tiny Archibald leap an amazing 6 ft. off the ground as he passes the ball to a teammate for a sure layup. 3 3-point plays by Archibald were recently cited by sportswriters who elected him to the All-Star team of the NBA. All 3 were scored against 7 footers clogging the middle and all 3 will go into the NBA Book of Records. Coach Bill Musselman has said of the nba's smaller players, "Good things come in small packages."

Punctuation

47 End Punctuation: Period, Question Mark, Exclamation Point, Independent Clauses

1. The period is used to terminate any sentence in which a statement or an exhortation is made or a command given.

Statement The frost is on the pumpkin.
Command Speak softly, and carry a big stick.
Exhortation Let us behave like gentlemen.

2. Question marks are used in direct questions, but not in indirect questions.

Direct Question Where are the clowns?
Indirect Question She wondered where the clowns were.

3. Exclamation points are used to express strong emotion. (Caution: They should be used sparingly.)

Exclamation "Author! Author!" shouted the opening night audience.

4. A sentence that contains two or more independent (main) clauses may be punctuated in one of three ways:

A. We can treat each clause as an independent sentence.

He likes New York in June. She likes the Boston Red Sox. They both like *spaghetti carbonara.*

B. We can connect each clause with a semicolon.

He likes New York in June; she likes the Boston Red Sox; they both like *spaghetti carbonara.*

C. We can connect each clause with commas, *provided that we are also using coordinate conjunctions.*

He likes New York in June, and she likes the Boston Red Sox, but they both like *spaghetti carbonara.*

5. If the independent clauses are very brief, they may be connected with a comma or a semicolon. (To be on the safe side, use the semicolon.)

Optional I like coffee; I like tea.
Optional I like coffee, I like tea.

6. When independent clauses are joined by a *conjunctive adverb* (*however, moreover, furthermore, therefore*), use a semicolon before, and a comma after, the adverb if it is the first word in the second clause. If the adverb is in the middle of the clause, use the semicolon to separate the clauses and enclose the adverb with commas.

Jack has suffered a number of financial losses; however, he has not lost his sense of humor.

The team is in first place; the coach, nevertheless, has increased the number of hours we must practice.

47   Exercise/END PUNCTUATION

A. Insert the correct punctuation in the following sentences:

1. Is the teacher charged with neglect of duty able to refute the charges
2. Last season he stole 87 bases Incredible
3. I move that Exhibit A be accepted as evidence
4. Harrington, is that you
5. They asked if there were any hot water
6. Can it have been more than forty years since Pearl Harbor
7. "Oy-vey" sighed Mrs. O'Brien "Saints be praised" exclaimed Mrs. Cohen
8. Charlie is a good mechanic but Pete is a better salesman
9. "Look The sky is falling" shouted Chicken Little
10. Who stole my purse
11. Who steals my purse steals trash
12. Jeepers creepers Where did you get those peepers
13. Let's pay the check and leave this place
14. When I asked him why he behaved that way, he asked me what business it was of mine
15. Whose side are you on

Independent Clauses

B. Insert the correct punctuation in the following sentences:

1. Phil was a gifted shortstop but he could never go to his right
2. It was England's finest hour never had so many owed so much to so few
3. He came he saw he lost
4. Bert is a good dancer moreover he's a very snappy dresser

5. George and I went to the movies Sara and Jane went shopping Larry and his cousin headed for the local poolroom
6. He read my poetry and he recommended that I major in accounting
7. He says he wants to live in Venice but I think he prefers Buffalo
8. Eat drink and be merry
9. He bought violets for her furs and rings for her fingers
10. He neither smokes nor drinks consequently he is in excellent condition
11. Ella sang Louis played and Fred danced
12. He used to be at the head of the class today however he is just an average student
13. Some people can forget but not forgive others can forgive but not forget
14. You're witty you're grand
15. Her performance was outstanding his was barely adequate

48 Internal Punctuation I: The Comma—Subordinate Clauses and Phrases

1. Use a comma after introductory clauses or phrases. When the introductory phrase is brief and the meaning clear, the comma may be omitted.

While I was on my way to see you, I ran into George.

Optional   After dinner we went to a play.
Optional   After dinner, we went to a play.

2. When a clause or phrase is inserted within a main clause, enclose it within commas.

Tony, although hampered by a lisp, is a fine singer.
The Hawks, when everyone is healthy, can beat any team in the league.

---

48   Exercise/THE COMMA I

A. In the sentences below, insert commas where necessary. If no comma is required, leave the sentence unmarked.

1. Whenever Clancy came into the bar a hush fell over the place.
2. I will be delighted although I'm not much of a dancer to go to the dance with you.
3. When the temperature goes up the beach becomes crowded.
4. Long regarded as one of the country's leading newspapers the Washington *Post* boasts an outstanding staff of reporters.
5. Unaccustomed as I am to public speaking I will make my remarks brief.
6. After lunch we played bridge.
7. According to Carl the fire broke out in the garage.
8. Born in a trunk in the Princess Theater she spent her entire life in show business.
9. If I were you I would avoid his company.
10. That horse can run when the weather is right like a champion.

11. My answer if I understand your question is that such an event could never occur.
12. When he wakes up in the morning the first thing he does is to put the coffee on the stove.
13. They showed up at the party having first stopped off at the florist's with a bouquet of roses.
14. Remember that politics is first and foremost the art of the possible.
15. My opinion as long as you asked is that the expedition has an excellent chance for success.

B. Convert the following pairs of sentences into one sentence containing a subordinate phrase or clause. Insert commas wherever they are required. If a comma is optional, place an O above the comma.

> *Example*   I saw him at the beach yesterday. He looked tired.
>
> When I saw him at the beach yesterday, he looked tired.

1. I was educated at a private high school. Therefore I learned quite a bit of grammar.

_____

_____

2. Please bring me fresh rolls from the bakery. Also stop at the cheese store and pick up some brie.

_____

_____

3. You are in the premedical program. You probably spend a great deal of time studying.

_____

_____

4. I am the spokesman for the student senate. I welcome you.

_____

_____

5. A. C. Bradley published *Shakespearean Tragedy* in 1904. Some felt that there was no longer anything to be said on the subject.

_____

_____

6. He was trained by a master carpenter. He really knows his craft.

_____

_____

7. I wish that you and I were alone now. I would tell you what I really think.

_____

_____

8. The explosion lasted only a few seconds. It destroyed the entire building.

_____

_____

9. I was taking an unusually large number of courses. At the same time I was working part time.

_____

_____

10. John loved to listen to Art Tatum's playing. John was trained as a classical pianist.

_____

_____

49 Internal Punctuation II: The Comma—Restrictive and Nonrestrictive Elements

Restrictive elements are those that provide essential information in the sentence. They are *not* set off by commas. Nonrestrictive elements are those that add information but that are not essential to the meaning of the main clause. Nonrestrictive items are set off by commas.

Restrictive The man who broke the bank at Monte Carlo was Chauncey Alcott.
Nonrestrictive Chauncey Alcott, the man who broke the bank at Monte Carlo, married my grandmother.

Note: Elements that describe proper nouns are generally nonrestrictive; "which" clauses in which the word *that* can be substituted for the word *which* without altering the meaning are generally restrictive.

Nonrestrictive Duquesne University, which is located in Pittsburgh, offers a program in humanistic psychology.
Restrictive The location which (that) I have in mind is in the southeastern section of town.

---

49 Exercise/THE COMMA II

A. The following sentences place commas around elements that are not essential. Sentences that contain restrictive elements should be left unmarked.

1. Bill Russell who used to coach the Boston Celtics is now a television sports commentator.
2. "You're the guy who gave it to my brother in the back."
3. The team which won the National League pennant in 1942 was the St. Louis Cardinals.
4. The Cardinals who entered the World Series as underdogs went on to win the Series in five games.
5. The class sleepy and bored looked at the teacher with glazed eyes.
6. He said he was from Brazil where the nuts come from.

7. Anyone caught cheating will be expelled.

8. The prisoner seeing the opportunity to escape ran for the open window.

9. That fellow whoever he is really knows how to play the trumpet.

10. The man sitting in the third row is a well-known drama critic.

11. My father who was a coal miner for thirty years was a dedicated union member.

12. My position which I arrived at after considerable reflection is that life is just a bowl of cherries.

13. Let those who think they can do better volunteer to be on the town council.

14. A person who knows how to use the media to advantage is a person who will go far in politics.

15. He was reelected from his congressional district thirteen times no mean feat.

B. Combine the following pairs of sentences into single sentences containing restrictive or nonrestrictive elements. Punctuate accordingly.

Nonrestrictive Example   Everyone is eligible. This is regardless of race, color, or creed.

Everyone, regardless of race, color, or creed, is eligible.

Restrictive Example   Some things happen for the first time. These things seem to have happened before.

Some things that happen for the first time seem to have happened before.

1. Sydney Greenstreet was a popular character actor in the 1940s. He played the rival café owner in *Casablanca*.

_____

_____

2. The service in a restaurant is as important as the food. The restaurant wishes to be considered first class.

_____

_____

3. The father raced into the burning building. The father was heedless of the danger.

_____

_____

4. People come to this hospital. These people have abandoned all hope.

_____

_____

5. Carol and Joan look like sisters. They frequently travel together.

_____

_____

6. My Aunt Rose has gone to California. She usually travels alone.

_____

_____

7. New Mexico State University is one of the great colleges of the American West. It has turned out some of the most accomplished people in the nation.

_____

_____

8. Car owners are now struggling with gas milage problems. They bought big gas guzzlers.

_____

_____

9. The man looks restless. He is wearing a blue suit and standing against the wall.

_____

_____

10. People shouldn't throw stones. They live in glass houses.

_____

_____

50 Internal Punctuation III: The Comma—Elements in a Series

1. Use commas to separate a series of words, phrases, or clauses. Although the placement of the comma before the conjunction at the end of the series is optional, it is preferable to use the comma.

In the valleys, in the hills, and in the villages of the district, the air was tense with anticipation of the impending invasion.
Violets, roses, peonies, and orange blossoms were among the many flowers in the hospital room.

2. Use the semicolon to separate the major elements, if these elements are themselves subdivided into smaller elements separated by commas.

He included among his many interests the following: the arts, music, dance, and painting; science, physics, biology, and chemistry; public affairs, government, politics, and social welfare.

50 Exercise/THE COMMA III

Insert the appropriate commas in the following sentences.

1. At dinner he had a cocktail a carafe of wine and an Irish coffee.
2. The winners of the beauty contest were as follows: Jean Kane a native of Delaware Ellen Frank who comes from Florida and Ann Boland a resident of New Jersey.
3. Quietly cautiously fearfully we advanced upon the enemy position.
4. Smiling sighing laughing crying he ran the gamut of emotions.
5. He said his four favorite composers were Bach Beethoven Berlioz and Berlin.
6. She typed the letter sealed it stamped it and placed it in the mail box.
7. He fought a clean hard honest fight.
8. His marriage his career even his life all of these were at stake as a result of that fateful decision.
9. Bill who had some experience in the theater was to be the director Joan a

student at a local design institute was to do the scenery and Mary who had starred in a high school production of *South Pacific* was to play the lead.

10. *Hamlet Henry V Coriolanus* and *The Tempest* were his favorite Shakespearean plays.

11. When the sun goes down when the tide comes in when the moon is high everyone in town comes down to the levee.

12. The women tall lean lovely were in the living room the men raucous noisy and laughing were in the basement.

13. Ted goes with Alice Sid with Samantha and you go with Fergus.

14. Hastily desperately and futilely Ellen tried to repair the broken plate.

15. Courage integrity honor and the love of women were the values for which he lived and died.

51 Internal Punctuation IV: The Comma—Appositives, Direct Address, and Parenthetical Expressions

1. *Appositive.* An appositive is a noun or noun phrase located next to another noun with which it is identified. An appositive is enclosed by commas.

Ann Taylor, my closest friend, advised me to take the job.
Hamlet, the Prince of Denmark, does not appear in the opening scene of the play.

2. *Restrictive appositive.* Some appositives are *not* set off by commas because they function the way restrictive elements do; that is, they provide the specific identity of the preceding noun.

The novel *Transatlantic Blues* was written by Wilfred Sheed.
My boy Bill will grow strong and tall.

3. *Direct address.* The name of someone to whom you are directly speaking is set off by commas.

Play it again, Sam.
I must say, Curt, that I am disappointed.

4. *Parenthetical expressions.* Words inserted into a sentence in order to clarify the speaker's intention are set off by commas.

His necktie, for example, is flamboyant.
It is, I'm afraid, too late to repent.

---

51 Exercise/THE COMMA IV

A. Insert commas where necessary in the following sentences. Be careful not to enclose restrictive appositives in commas.

1. Uncle George a notorious rake is wanted by the police of two continents.

2. He gave Fred one of his nephews a bad check.

3. What we need is new leadership leadership that will seize opportunity rather than react to problems.

4. He is in my opinion not qualified for the job.

5. "There are more things in heaven and earth Horatio than are dreamt of in your philosophy."

6. Let Nancy our most skilled speaker represent us at the conference.

7. He moved from Brooklyn the former home of the Dodgers to Los Angeles the Dodgers' present home.

8. Other characters in the play include Kent Lear's faithful follower and Edgar Gloucester's legitimate son.

9. In the view of some critics it is Edgar who delivers the play's most significant line "Ripeness is all."

10. The N train the express to Coney Island and the A train the express to Rockaway Beach were particularly crowded on that hot sunny day.

11. Burt your problem I really feel is that you lack patience to see a task to its conclusion.

12. "The fault dear Brutus lies not in our stars but in ourselves."

13. You Jack Bierstad had the opportunity and the motive to commit the crime.

B. Combine the pairs of sentences below into single sentences containing appositives.

> *Example*   He wore the sign of victory. The sign of victory was a laurel wreath.
>
> He wore a laurel wreath, the sign of victory.

1. Ellen has fallen in love with Mike. Ellen is a union organizer; Mike is an FBI agent.

_____

_____

2. Saul Bellow and Gwendolyn Brooks live in Chicago. He is a famous novelist; she is a distinguished poet.

_____

_____

3. "America" was written by Leonard Bernstein and Stephen Sondheim. "America" is a song from the musical *West Side Story*.

_____

_____

4. We all miss Lenny. Lenny served in our club as the voice of reason.

_____

5. Eisenhower and Grant were victorious generals. They were each elected President after the wars in which they served.

_____

52 Exercise/PUNCTUATION REVIEW TEST I:
END PUNCTUATION

In the following sentences insert the appropriate periods, question marks, and exclamation points. When the sentence is compound, place commas and semicolons as needed between independent clauses.

1. Oops The plate slipped from my hands
2. When are we scheduled to leave
3. How many people are invited to the wedding and how many will be coming to the reception
4. Henry Kissinger was Secretary of State in the Nixon and Ford administrations Dean Rusk held the same position in the Kennedy administration
5. Wow Did you see what I saw
6. "Great" he exclaimed when he was told of his team's victory
7. See no evil speak no evil hear no evil
8. June preferred to listen to classical music Ben favored hard rock
9. "Whose pocketbook is this" she asked
10. He said goodnight to Irene but he did not go straight home
11. People are driving fewer cars and getting better mileage and spending less money on gas
12. Did you say that the medium was speaking to someone who has been dead for ten years Impossible
13. Paris was her favorite city therefore "April in Paris" was her favorite song
14. Quit He doesn't know the meaning of the word
15. What has become of Sally
16. He wondered what became of Sally
17. It was General McAuliffe who replied "Nuts" to the German demand for surrender
18. He believed in himself but he lacked faith in his partner
19. "Dee-fense" shouted the excited crowd as the home team clung to its one-point lead
20. He tried singing in the rain he tried dancing in the dark but nothing could cure his melancholy

53 Exercise/PUNCTUATON REVIEW TEST II: INTERNAL PUNCTUATION

A. In the sentences below, insert the appropriate commas and semicolons.

1. My address 99 Bank Street is right across the street from Hernando's Hideaway a local bistro.
2. At our last meeting we spoke of the duties responsibilities and opportunities of the position.
3. "Friends Romans Countrymen lend me your ears."
4. "You naughty kittens you've lost your mittens."
5. The witness Dr. Lemback affirmed that he had never met the defendant George Rogers.
6. Will this opinion provocative as it is be sustained by the Appelate Court the highest court in the state?
7. In 1601 Essex the most charismatic figure in London led a revolt against his former protector Queen Elizabeth.
8. Her mother's name was Mary a grand old name.
9. When the witness first took the stand the courtroom was abnormally quiet.
10. "When a man's an empty kettle he should be on his mettle yet I'm torn apart."

B. Insert the appropriate commas and semicolons in the following paragraphs.

Now that he was a successful businessman Roger Sands looked back at the early days of his career with a certain not nostalgia exactly but warmth. In those days the early fifties he was living in a two-room walk-up apartment. Sometimes he was so short of cash that he would have to borrow money to get to his job at the American Veil Company. The company located at 37th Street and 7th Avenue in the heart of New York's garment district manufactured bridal veils and Roger's job consisted of pushing a hand truck through the noisy crowded bustling streets delivering veils to local wholesalers. The work was difficult the pay poor the boss a sharp-tongued perfectionist who showed only one emotion disdain. Nevertheless Roger was happy. He was young and healthy he was learning the business and most important he was in love. Her name was Maggie she worked for a dress company across the street from his. Every day they would meet for lunch. Weather permitting they would bring their bag lunches over to Herald Square sit on one of the benches and talk about their future. Looking back Roger would often think that he had never been happier than he was during those lunch hours sipping a Coke eating a ham and cheese on a roll and looking at Maggie.

Born in 1960 the year John F. Kennedy was elected President Stephanie Granger began life in Carbondale Illinois. When Stephanie was eight years old her family moved to Oak Forest a suburb of Chicago. Stephanie who early showed signs of athletic talent starred on the volleyball and basketball teams of her local high school James Madison High. When it came time for college she was recruited by a number of schools included among which were Ohio State Michigan Rutgers and Southern Illinois which is located in Carbondale. After carefully weighing the advantages and disadvantages of each school Stephanie a top student as well as a fine athlete chose Southern Illinois. Why? "Well it's like this" she explained to her coach Rose Macaulay "At heart I suppose I'm really a homebody."

54 Quotation Marks

1. Use quotation marks to report the exact words of a speaker or writer. If, at the end of the quotation, a period or comma is required, it is placed within the quotation; if a semicolon or colon is needed, it should be placed outside the quotation.

The headline read: "Three Die in Auto Crash."
He declared, "I'm not guilty," but the jury did not believe him.
I said, "We're going to win"; I've always been an optimist.

2. Use a comma when a direct quotation is interrupted to indicate the speaker or writer.

"Something there is," wrote Robert Frost, "that doesn't love a wall."

3. Place a question mark inside the quotation marks if it applies only to the quotation. Place it outside if it applies to the whole sentence.

"Who is it?" she called.
She called, "Who is it?"
Did she ask, "Who is it"?

4. Use quotation marks for titles of essays, poems, short stories, and songs. Titles of books, films, and plays should be underlined (italicized in print), not placed within quotation marks.

The song "Lucky in Love" is from the film *Good News*.
Flannery O'Connor's short story "Judgment Day" appears in her collection of
  stories *Everything That Rises Must Converge*.

5. Use quotation marks to call attention to the word or phrase you are using.

What's good about "good-bye"?

6. Use a single quotation mark to enclose a quotation within a quotation.

"As a child I was known as 'chubby,' " he declared.

54 Exercise/PUNCTUATION: QUOTATION MARKS AND OTHERS

In the following sentences insert the appropriate quotation marks, periods, commas, semicolons, and question marks.

1. In the last scene of the film Gladys George while cradling the dead body of James Cagney looks up at the policeman and says He used to be a big shot

2. Everybody as Jimmy Durante used to say wants to get into the act

3. His article Supply Side Economics was reprinted in three major newspapers

4. Where do you think you're going she demanded

5. When Hamlet's mother asks him Why seems it so particular with thee he replies Seems Madam Nay it is I know not seems

6. Who was it who said Dr. Livingston I presume

7. It's a quarter to three is the opening line of One for My Baby a song by Harold Arlen and Johnny Mercer

8. Put out the light says Othello as he prepares to murder Desdemona And then put out the light

9. When I said Come early Jack hastily explained I didn't mean three hours before the gates opened

10. The award winner's acceptance speech was brief: As George M Cohan would say My mother thanks you my father thanks you and I thank you

55 The Apostrophe

1. Use the apostrophe to show possession.

Paul's hat   baby's skin
car's performance   company's reputation

2. If a singular noun ends in -*s*, add the apostrophe and -*s* when the word is short—one or two syllables. If the word contains more than two syllables simply add an apostrophe.

James's hat   bus's motor
class's behavior   Yeats's poetry

but

Aristophanes' plays   psychoanalysis' expense

3. Add the apostrophe after the -*s* for words that form their plural with an -*s* or -*es*.

the boys' games
the Joneses' party

4. Add apostrophe -*s* to plural nouns not ending in -*s*.

children's clothes
women's rights

5. Do *not* use the apostrophe with possessive pronouns: *its, yours, hers, his, theirs, ours, whose.*

Note: it's a contraction for *it is;* never use *it's* as a possessive pronoun.

6. Add an apostrophe -*s* to indicate the plurals of numbers and letters.

There are four i's in Mississippi.
His favorite decade was the 1960's.

7. Use an apostrophe in contraction to show the omission of certain letters.

can't (cannot)   you're (you are)
they're (they are)   he's (he is)

In the following sentences, insert apostrophes as needed.

1. Im just a gal who cant say no.
2. The childs role in the school pageant was to play the Spirit of 76 as represented by the Class of 88.
3. His bachelors degree was from one of the countrys best universities.
4. The Smiths relatives visit them every spring; the Joneses relatives every fall.
5. Jacks store specializes in mens clothing.
6. My brother-in-laws job is with the attorney-general's office.
7. He minds his ps and qs around VIPs.
8. Although he was a star in the 1980s, as late as the 1940s he was performing for GIs in Europe.
9. The ERAs passage is still in doubt; the CIAs budget is still a secret, as is the IRAs leadership.
10. France and Englands agreement was offset by Germany and Japans secret pact.

56 The Hyphen

The hyphen is used to:

divide a word at the end of a line (following dictionary syllabication).

I was very deep in conversation with Judy.

join together words or prefixes and words.

self-service	ex-President
all-purpose	great-grandfather
air-brake	merry-go-round

join a prefix to a proper noun.

anti-Nixon   un-American   pro-Reagan

join a prefix ending in a vowel to a word beginning with the same vowel.

anti-intellectual	re-educate
co-ordinate	de-escalate
pre-election	

join a prefix to a word to discriminate between words.

recreation—re-creation   reprove—re-prove

low-level official   *devil-may-care* attitude   *fence-busting* outfielder

join compound numbers from twenty-one to ninety-nine and specifying fractions.

seventy-seven   two-fifths

Note: When compound adjectives are used as predicate adjectives, the hyphens are omitted.

He is out of work.

---

56 Exercise/CORRECT USE OF THE HYPHEN

In the following list, some words are given in their correct form; others require hyphens. Write *C* next to the correct items. Rewrite those that require hyphens.

1. Son of Sam _____

2. x ray _____

3. unambitious _____

4. antiseptic _____

5. prolranian _____

6. semi professional _____

7. deemphasize _____

8. dissatisfy _____

9. ninetyfour _____

10. threesevenths _____

11. wildeyed _____

12. selfsatisfied _____

13. AllAmerican _____

14. reeducate _____

15. sevenninths _____

16. twentyeight _____

17. cavein _____

18. beesting _____

19. quasiinvalid _____

20. ablebodied seaman _____

57 The Dash and the Colon

Use the colon to set up an explanation, a long quotation, or a list. It is frequently used after the words *the following* or *as follows*.

The answer is simple: The system has failed.
He needs the following: food, shelter, clothing, and a decent cigar.

Use the colon to separate the hour and minute when indicating the time, and to indicate chapter and verse in the Bible.

3:40 a.m.   Genesis 6:10

Use the dash to set off material that interrupts the sentence or to set off a final appositive that contains commas within it.

He was appalled—and I do mean appalled—at the prospect of living in that apartment.
Three members of the graduating class were accepted to law school—Jane, Joan, and Jacqueline.

For exercises on the use of the dash and the colon, see Section 58.

58 Parentheses and Brackets

Use parentheses to set off material that adds incidental or supplementary information. The use of either parentheses or dash marks is frequently optional.

His friend (I should say his acquaintance; he had no friends), John Long, used to
    say that he was a bear in the morning and a tiger at night.

Use brackets to insert a word or phrase within a quotation.

He testified, "When I first met the defendant [George Brandt] he was working
    on the stock exchange.

---

58 Exercise/PARENTHESES AND BRACKETS

In the following sentences, insert hyphens, dashes, colons, parentheses, or brackets where needed.

1. He expects us would you believe this to write a 500 word essay every week.
2. He wrote a well remembered tribute to his long lost brother.
3. The result of that early effort was seen in his later life he became a much loved family physician.
4. He lived if you would call that living on the south side of town.
5. The Modern Language Association MLA has its headquarters in New York.
6. George told me, "If you see him George's brother Bill in Chicago, give him my regards."
7. My father came home one evening I remember that it had rained and his clothes were soaking wet to announce that we were moving to St. Louis.
8. The first song they wrote "Any Old Place with You" was an immediate success.
9. Among Walker Percy's many novels are the following *The Moviegoer, Lancelot, Love Among the Ruins,* and *The Second Coming.*
10. In *The Great Santini,* Robert Duvall plays a marine pilot a macho daredevil who is a stern but loving family man.

11. The waiter he had grown up on the same street as I came over to where I was sitting and shook my hand.
12. I am enclosing thirty dollars $30.
13. George you know old George put a lampshade on his head at the height of the party.
14. Winning the game, winning the girl, and winning the sweepstakes all these made Phil feel that life was worth living after all.
15. He had one piece of advice for everyone he met "Invest in plastics."

59 Exercise/PUNCTUATION REVIEW TEST III

A. The sentences below contain letters in the spaces where a particular type of punctuation should be. In the corresponding space to the right, place the correct punctuation mark.

Example   When George returns (A) tell him that the children will be home at five (B) they are staying late at school (C)

A ____,____
B ____;____
C ____.____

1. What they say about Dixie (A) is it true (B)

A _____
B _____

2. In the civics course I took last year (A) you know, the one Ms. Henley taught—I learned all about the legislative, judicial (B) and executive branches (C)

A _____
B _____
C _____

3. Sara Jackman (A) how (B)s by you (C)

A _____
B _____
C _____

4. His list of the all (A) time great motion picture stars included the following (B) Garbo, Chaplin, Tracy, Hepburn (C) and Brando.

A _____
B _____
C _____

5. We will be in Pittsburgh by nightfall (A) that (B) at least (C) is our plan.

A _____
B _____
C _____

6. According to the printed rules (A) "The game may be played by any number of players, from two to six" (B) I know from experience (C) however (D) that four is the ideal number.

A _____
B _____
C _____
D _____

7. "What was the real name of the man known as Leadbelly (A) (B) asked June (C)

A _____
B _____
C _____

8. Who(A)s charged with determining whose rights have been violated (B)

A _____
B _____

9. Last night we saw a play about Casey Stengel (A) the play focused on Casey(B)s unique relationship with the English language (C) a relationship that produced the hybrid known as "Stengelese" (D)

A _____
B _____
C _____
D _____

10. *Variety* (A) the show business newspaper, announced the collapse of the stock market in 1929 with the following headline (B) "WALL STREET LAYS AN EGG (C) (D)

A _____
B _____
C _____
D _____

B. Punctuate the sentence reproduced below:

We the people of the United States in order to form a more perfect union establish justice insure domestic tranquility provide for the common defense promote the general welfare and secure the blessings of liberty to ourselves and our posterity do ordain and establish this Constitution for the United States of America.

C. Punctuate the following:

Fourscore and seven years ago our fathers brought forth upon this continent a new nation conceived in liberty and dedicated to the proposition that all men are created equal. Now we are engaged in a great civil war testing whether that nation or any nation so conceived so dedicated can long endure . . . . It is rather for us to be here dedicated to the great task remaining before us . . . that we here highly resolve that these dead shall not have died in vain that this nation under God shall have a new birth of freedom and that government of the people by the people and for the people shall not perish from the earth.

Diction

60 Using the Dictionary

The dictionary is a wonderful but wholly underutilized book. Most of us use it to look up either the meaning or the proper spelling of a word. And the latter pursuit is likely to be a chore when you don't know the proper spelling because locating the word depends on what you don't know!

In addition to definitions and spelling, the dictionary provides a wealth of information—all of which when properly absorbed contributes to a writer's sharpened sense of language, his or her capacity to use words accurately, spell them properly, divide them, remember their relevance to other words, and a great deal more.

Dictionary entries provide the following information:

1. Pronunciation—sometimes several acceptable ones for each word.
2. Spelling, with any significant and acceptable variants.
3. Syllabication, the proper way to divide a word at the end of a line of text.
4. For verbs, the principal parts.
5. For nouns, the proper plural forms.
6. The etymology of the word: a tracing back to its origins.
7. The part or parts of speech to which the word usually belongs.
8. Hyphenation, the up-to-date convention regarding compound words.
9. Capitalization, the latest practice of educated professionals.
10. The meaning of prefixes and suffixes.
11. Synonyms.
12. Other information.
13. Meanings.

60 Exercise/USING THE DICTIONARY

A. Get out your dictionary and read through the key to pronunciation symbols. Next, read carefully through the section called user's guide to the dictionary or reader's guide to the dictionary. As you do this, keep at your side the list of informational items given on the previous page so that you may familiarize yourself with what your guide says about these matters.

Now, consult the dictionary on the following words. Read each entry carefully. Find out all you can about each word. At the end of two or three study sessions with the dictionary guides, the list on the previous page, and these words, you should be more at ease than not in a dictionary entry.

1. satrap	6. tuxedo	11. taskforce	16. index
2. acrimonious	7. recondite	12. judgment	17. thrive
3. esthetic	8. kodak	13. artefact	18. locus
4. exculpate	9. roseola	14. bowdlerize	19. picaresque
5. aggravate	10. diverticulosis	15. beriberi	20. alumna

B. Answer the following questions about the words listed above:

1. What is the plural of *alumna*? Of *index*? _____

2. What is the derivation of *picaresque*? _____

3. What does *exculpate* mean? _____

4. Use *exculpate* in a sentence. _____
_____

5. How do you pronounce *recondite*? _____

6. Divide *diverticulosis* into syllables. _____

7. Is *artefact* spelled correctly? _____

8. Should *kodak* be capitalized? _____

9. What is the derivation of *tuxedo*? _____

10. What is the past participle of *thrive*? _____

11. Is there any other way to spell *esthetic*? _____

12. Use *aggravate* in a sentence. _____
_____

13. Is there only one way to spell *judgment*? _____

14. How does *satrap* get its name? _____

15. Can *taskforce* be hyphenated? _____

16. What is the plural of *locus*? _____

17. What is the derivation of *beriberi*? _____

_____

18. In pronouncing *acrimonious*, where does the main accent fall? _____

61 Vocabulary Building I: Prefixes and Suffixes

One way to build your vocabulary is to familiarize yourself with common *prefixes*, syllables that precede words, and *suffixes*, syllables that are tacked on to the end of words. If you know the meaning of a prefix or suffix, you can frequently figure out the meaning of a strange word. Moreover, knowing these meaningful syllables can help you to form new words and thus expand your vocabulary.

Prefixes	Meaning	Sample Words
a-, an-	without, not	amoral, abyss, anarchy
ab-, abs-	off, away from	absent, aberrant
ad- (ac-, ag-, al-, an-, as-, at-)	to (the basic form *ad-* changes to one of the others before certain consonants)	admit, adapt, accept
ante-	before in space or time	antedate, antebellum
anti-	against, opposed to, opposite	antibody, anticlerical
bi-	twice, two	bisect, biweekly
circum-	around	circumnavigate, circumvent
com- (con-, co-, cog-, col-, cor-)	together or with (the basic form *com-* changes to the others before root words with certain consonants)	commute, commit, confer, cohabit, cooperate
contra-	against, opposing, opposite	contradict, controversy
de-	from, off, down	detract, debar, descend
demi-	half	demitasse
dia-	across, through, thorough	diagonal, dialogue
dis- (dif-, di-)	apart, away, not (the basic form *dis-* changes to *dif-* before roots beginning with *f-* and changes also to *di-* before certain other consonants)	disappear, dissect, differ, digest
ex-, e-	from, out of, thoroughly (the basic form *ex-* changes to *e-* before certain consonants)	except, expel, emit

Prefixes	Meaning	Sample Words
extra-, extro-	outside, beyond	extrovert, extravagant, extrapolate
in- (im-, il-, ir-)	not (the basic form *in-* changes to the others before certain consonants)	inhuman, impossible
inter-, intro-	between, among, together	interstella, introduce
mal-	bad, wrong	malcontent, malicious
mis-	ill, wrong	mistake, mischance
non-	not	nonconformist
ob- (oc-, of-, ob-)	toward, against, to, on, over (the basic *ob-* changes to the others before certain consonants)	objective, offend, occlude
pre-	before, earlier	prevent, precede, preclude
pro-	pro, forward	pro-Labor, proceed
re-	again, back	renew, repeat, restart
sub- (suc-, suf-, sug-, sup-, sur-)	under (the basic form *sub-* changes before certain consonants)	submarine, suggest, suppose, suffer
super-, sur-	over, in spatial size or quality	superman, superviser, surround
trans-	across, beyond	transport, transfer
un-	not, reversal	undo, unnecessary, unfasten, unadorn

Suffixes can also help you to build your vocabulary. Notice, as you read this list, how new words are formed by the addition of suffixes and how a new part of speech is sometimes created in the process.

Suffix	Meaning	Sample Words
-ac	pertaining to	insomniac, cardiac
-al	relating to	aural, oral
-ance	state or quality of	distance, sustenance
-ancy	state or quality of	hesitancy, relevancy
-ant	quality of	defiant, dormant
-ant	one who	defendant
-arium	a place for something	planetarium, terrarium
-ary	a place for something	commissary
-ate	to cause	educate, graduate
-ation	cause or act of causing	elevation, hibernation
-ative	tendency, inclination	negative, procreative
-cy	state or quality of	solvency
-cy	office	presidency
-dom	state of, quality of	freedom
-ee	one who receives an action	legatee, donee
-eer	one who	mutineer, privateer
-en	constructed of	wooden, molten
-en	to make	shorten, widen, lengthen
-ence	state or quality of	affluence

Suffix	Meaning	Sample Words
-er	one who, that which	worker, carpenter, rubber
-er	more	happier
-escence	state of beginning to be	convalescent
-esque	resembling in a special style	picturesque, burlesque
-ess	female performer of action	actress, mistress
-est	most	finest, best
-et, -ette	diminutive	cigarette
-ful	full of	wishful
-hood	state of, quality of	childhood
-ian	belonging to	Armenian
-ible	capable of	irresistible
-ic	belonging or pertaining to	systemic, Homeric
-ic	concerning, characterized by	comic, hysteric
-ice	state or quality of	avarice
-ion	state of, act of	creation, confusion
-ish	resembling	boyish
-ism	state of being	heroism, communism
-ive	characterized by	superlative
-ize	to do or make	hypnotize
-like	resembling	childlike
-ment	state, result of making	merriment, abandonment
-ness	state or quality of	happiness, tenderness
-oid	resembling	humanoid
-or	one who	captor, censor
-or	state of	humor, languor
-orium	a place for	auditorium
-ory	a place for	lavatory, laboratory
-ose	full of, like	grandiose, verbose
-osis	state of, disease	hypnosis, meiosis
-ous	filled with	nervous, delicious
-ry	quality, condition	heraldry, thievery
-ship	state or quality of	friendship
-tion	state or result of	condition
-tude	quality of	lassitude, pulchritude
-ty	state of	humility
-ure	result of, condition, organization	nature, exposure, pressure

61 Exercise/WORKING WITH PREFIXES AND SUFFIXES TO BUILD VOCABULARY

A. Add an appropriate prefix to each of the following words to create a new word with a negative meaning. Then write two sentences using each of the new words. Writing the sentences will help establish the word in your vocabulary.

Example   satiable _____insatiable_____ (new word)
             a. The dog's appetite was insatiable. _____
             b. He looked like an insatiable eater. _____

(Note that the word is used in two different positions in the sentence, that is, as a predicate adjective and as an adjective modifying a noun. Try to use the words in sentences as this one is, that is, in different positions.)

1. divided _____ (new word)

     a. _____

     b. _____

2. swimmer _____ (new word)

     a. _____

     b. _____

3. stable _____ (new word)

     a. _____

     b. _____

4. dramatic _____ (new word)

     a. _____

     b. _____

5. conscious _____ (new word)

     a. _____

     b. _____

6. believer _____ (new word)

    a. _____

    b. _____

7. decisive _____ (new word)

    a. _____

    b. _____

8. discovered _____ (new word)

    a. _____

    b. _____

9. frequent _____ (new word)

    a. _____

    b. _____

10. embark _____ (new word)

    a. _____

    b. _____

Note: Be sure to look up the new words in the dictionary if you do not know to what part of speech they belong. This will help you in writing sentences.

B. Add an appropriate suffix to each of the words below to create a new word having as part of its meaning *an act or state of* or *quality of.* After you've made the new word, check the dictionary to be sure you've spelled it correctly, since the addition of a suffix can frequently change a word's spelling. After the word is spelled correctly, use it in a sentence.

    Example   Fragment _____fragmentary_____ (new word)
            (sentence) His story was fragmentary. _____

1. child _____ (new word)

    (sentence) _____

_____

2. kind _____ (new word)

(sentence) _____

_____

3. guardian _____ (new word)

(sentence) _____

_____

4. conscious _____ (new word)

(sentence) _____

_____

5. repair _____ (new word)

(sentence) _____

_____

6. motive _____ (new word)

(sentence) _____

_____

7. consider _____ (new word)

(sentence) _____

_____

8. battle _____ (new word)

(sentence) _____

_____

9. determined _____ (new word)

(sentence) _____

_____

10. argue _____ (new word)

(sentence) _____

_____

62 Vocabulary Building II: Establishing New Word Meanings

Looking up the meaning of the word in a dictionary will not help to establish that word in your vocabulary, that is to say, establish the word in the basic stock you have available to use at any one moment. Even writing the meaning down in a notebook is of little value. There are only two things that will help:

1. Using the new word in a sentence in as many ways as you can. That is, an adjective should be used as a predicate adjective and as the modifier of a noun; a noun should be used as subject, object, object of a preposition, and so forth.
2. Using the new word in your speech wherever possible, until such time as you feel it to be comfortable and familiar.

Whoever plans to build his or her vocabulary should embark on the project as an ongoing discipline and try to acquire new words in a regular way. Many books are available which will provide you with lists of new words of graduated difficulty. Consult a good one for a plan to follow.

---

62 Exercise/ESTABLISHING NEW WORD MEANINGS

A. Look up in your dictionary each of the words given below. Read the definitions. Print the parts of speech the dictionary assigns to each. Then for each word and each function suggested, write at least two sentences.

Example   chagrin *n.* mental uneasiness caused by failure, disappointment or humbled pride; *v.t.* to cause anguish by disappointment or humiliation (chiefly in passive voice).

n. The chagrin I felt when she turned me down was more than I could talk about.
v.t. He was chagrined when he learned he'd failed math.

1. altruistic _____

_____

_____

_____

2. ambient _____

_____

_____

3. ameliorate _____

_____

_____

_____

4. androgynous _____

_____

_____

_____

_____

5. anomalous _____

_____

_____

_____

6. aplomb _____

_____

_____

_____

7. assiduous _____

_____

_____

_____

8. assuage _____

_____

_____

_____

9. banal _____

_____

_____

_____

10. bellicose _____

_____

_____

_____

11. castigate _____

_____

_____

_____

12. cogent _____

_____

_____

_____

13. collusion _____

_____

_____

_____

14. convivial _____

_____

_____

_____

15. covert _____

_____

_____

_____

16. cursory _____

_____

_____

_____

17. denigrate _____

_____

_____

_____

18. derogatory _____

_____

_____

_____

284

19. diaphanous _____

_____

_____

_____

20. diatribe _____

_____

_____

_____

21. discourse _____

_____

_____

_____

22. disparage _____

_____

_____

_____

23. disparate _____

_____

_____

_____

24. emanate _____

_____

_____

_____

25. fatuous _____

_____

_____

_____

26. gesticulate _____

_____

_____

_____

27. gregarious _____

_____

_____

_____

28. implicit _____

_____

_____

_____

29. ingenuous _____

_____

_____

_____

30. moribund _____

_____

_____

_____

31. myopic _____

_____

_____

_____

32. penchant _____

_____

_____

_____

33. punctilious _____

_____

_____

_____

34. reticent _____

_____

_____

_____

35. repudiate _____

_____

_____

_____

36. subterfuge _____

_____

_____

_____

37. tangible _____

_____

_____

_____

38. untenable _____

_____

_____

_____

39. usurp _____

_____

_____

_____

40. vacuous _____

_____

_____

_____

63 Vocabulary Building III: Synonymy

One or more words that mean essentially but not exactly the same thing are called *synonyms*. The writer who is aware of and chooses to work with synonyms can expand his or her vocabulary and make it more accurate by achieving a subtle command of groups of synonyms.

A good desk dictionary discriminates between synonyms in explanatory passages (labeled *Synonyms* or *Syns.*) which normally follow the definitions of a main-entry word. These passages are sometimes called synonymies, but they do not always occur in the dictionary where you look for them. If you cannot find the synonymy after the particular word you look up, you will more often than not find that the entry refers you to the proper word following which the synonymy appears.

There are also dictionaries solely devoted to synonymies, as well as mere listings of synonyms given in books called thesauruses.

Here is a sample synonymy from *The American Heritage Dictionary of the American Language* (p. 255a):

Synonyms: coarse, gross, crass, indelicate, vulgar, obscene, ribald. These adjectives primarily describe offensive speech or writing or behavior. *Coarse* implies roughness and crudeness in manners, appearance or expression. *Gross* implies excessive behavior approaching bestiality. *Crass* suggests stupidity combined with rudeness or other manifestation of lack of refinement: *crass ignorance. Indelicate* implies immodesty, tactless behavior, or lack of taste in expression: *an indelicate remark. Vulgar* emphasizes offensiveness to propriety and suggests boorishness and poor breeding. *Obscene* strongly stresses lewdness or indecency, particulary in reference to accepted standards of morality. *Ribald* implies vulgar, coarse, off-color language or behavior, intended to provoke laughter.

63 Exercise/DISCRIMINATING AMONG SYNONYMS

Below are groups of synonyms. Look up the meaning of each group, preferably in the synonymy in your dictionary. In the event that your dictionary does not include the group in a synonymy, look up the words separately. Then write sentences in which you use and clearly differentiate the various meanings of the words.

Example

excel   Mary excelled in science studies.

surpass   My professor surpasses me in knowledge but not in motivation.

exceed   The policeman exceeded his authority.

My wealth exceeds Janet's.

transcend   Great art transcends all possibility of explanation.

outdo   In his violin performance tonight, Peter outdid himself.

outstrip   In the mile race, Earl easily outstripped his rivals.

1. excessive

exorbitant

immoderate

extravagant

_____

_____

2. provoke

_____

_____

incite

_____

_____

stimulate

_____

_____

arouse

_____

_____

3. rely

_____

_____

trust

_____

_____

depend

_____

_____

bank

_____

_____

count

_____

_____

4. like

_____

_____

love

_____

_____

enjoy

_____

_____

relish

_____

_____

fancy

_____

_____

dote

_____

_____

5. adversary

_____

_____

opponent

_____

_____

foe

_____

_____

enemy

_____

_____

antagonist

_____

_____

6. sign

_____

_____

badge

_____

_____

mark

_____

_____

token

_____

_____

indication

_____

_____

symptom

_____

_____

64 Using Specific Language

Specific language is relatively more concrete than general language.

General	More Specific	Even More Specific
vehicle	automobile	Chevrolet
meat	poultry	chicken
clothing	trousers	blue jeans
foliage	tree	oak

In most cases, specific language is most useful. It imparts to your writing vividness and freshness because it gives a reader the opportunity to picture what you're saying.

64 Exercise/CHOOSING SPECIFIC LANGUAGE

For each of the italicized words in the sentences given below, find at least two more specific words or expressions and rewrite the sentence.

1. He *slept* for half an hour, then got up and ate some *food.*

   _____

   _____

2. He *walked* lazily down to the corner store.

   _____

   _____

3. I awoke to find an *animal* peeking into the window of the cabin.

   _____

   _____

4. I awoke to find a raccoon *looking into* the window of the cabin.

_____

_____

5. I like the taste of *fruit*.

_____

_____

6. She *ran* all the way home.

_____

_____

7. The man and his wife *fought* over money.

_____

_____

8. It was a *gray* day.

_____

_____

9. He really *wanted* a new pair of running shoes.

_____

_____

10. Alan didn't want to *show* his feelings.

_____

_____

11. He *came out* of the car.

12. She *called* for help.

13. She *read* the book.

14. They *worked* hard.

15. He is *sick.*

16. He is a *construction worker.*

17. The front yard was *full of* debris.

18. We had *fish* for dinner.

_____

_____

19. The car is *old*.

_____

_____

20. He likes the *water*.

_____

_____

65 Precise Expression I: Using Correct Idioms

An *idiom* is a customary form of expression; neither logic nor the dictionary meaning of a word can help you with it. Correct idioms must simply be learned. Here is a brief list of troublesome idiomatic combinations:

absolved by, from	I was absolved by the court. I was absolved from blame.
accompany by, on	I was accompanied by Tom. I was accompanied on my trip by Tom.
acquitted of	He was acquitted of all charges.
argue with, for, against, about	I argued with Harry about air pollution; he argued for and I argued against government controls.
compare to, with	Compared tome, he's a saint. He compared a small car with a big one.
communicate with, about	The two countries communicated about the border incident. I asked him to communicate with me.
confide in, to	Can I confide in you? I want to confide to you that I once broke the law.
connect by, with	The hose is connected by a coupling. I am connected with the Modern Language Association.
correspond to, with	I correspond with my colleagues regularly. A French province corresponds to an American state.
describe as, to	It was described as a blessing. I described to him my troubles with math.
differ about, from, with	We differ about the best wine to drink with fish. My ideas differ from his. I beg to differ with you.
different from*	My plans are very different from yours.
free from, of	We were free of him at last. I need to be freed from my obligations.

Different than is the colloquial usage when a clause is the object of the prepositional phrase.

Colloquial The farm looks different than I had expected.
Formal The farm looks different from what I had expected.

identical with	Your hat is identical to mine.
independent of	He is independent of his family.
live in, at, on	He lives at 525 East 89th Street, in an elegant mansion, on a private income.
necessity for, of	The necessary for vitamins has been established. There is no necessity of your catching a cold.
object to	I don't object to your statement.
overcome by, with	Sarah was overcome by sadness. John was overcome with admiration.
preferable to	To gourmets, veal is preferable to beef.
vary from, in, with	Ideas vary from one another just as shoe sizes vary in width. My mood varies with changes in the weather.

Idiomatic expression also requires that some verbs be followed by a gerund and some by an infinitive. Here is a brief list:

Infinitive	Gerund
able to go	capable of going
like to go	enjoy going
eager to go	cannot help going
hesitate to go	privilege of going
need to go	purpose of going
ask to go	consider going
consent to go	deny going
want to go	put off going

65 Exercise/USING CORRECT IDIOMS

Fill in with the correct idiomatic expression each of the blanks in the sentences below. If you cannot find the correct form on these pages, consult your dictionary.

1. We entered _____ a contract; therefore, we were legally

   connected _____ each other.

2. He was not capable of _____ to the hospital by himself,

   but he was persuaded _____ the necessity

   _____ .

3. The house was described _____ a lemon, but we con-

   sented _____ see it anyway.

4. Since we were free _____ academic obligations, we could consider _____ to the beach for a week, accompanied _____ Jim and Sarah.

5. We argued _____ the imposition of increased dormitory charges even though they do correspond roughly _____ charges at other schools.

6. He denied [use a form of *lose*] _____ the keys to the cottage but John did not absolve him _____ blame.

7. Paris looks different _____ I had expected but I enjoyed [use a form of *visit*] _____ every nook and cranny of it.

8. Living _____ the land teaches one independence.

9. After we had talked to the drunk for about twenty minutes, he consented [use a form of *leave*] _____ but he was overcome _____ regret.

10. I would compare the statue _____ a giant rock formation.

11. Our Declaration of Independence corresponds _____ the English Magna Carta.

I beg to differ _____ you.

13. Is there a parallel _____ the Vietnam War and the situation today in El Salvador?

14. Automobiles vary _____ one another _____ efficiency of combustion.

15. He acceded _____ the landlord's demands and moved the elephant out of his garage.

16. Going to summer school is preferable _____ working on a construction job.

17. She was bored _____ the reading assignments in her science fiction course.

18. He had a need [use a form of *perform*] _____ like a clown every time he saw her.

19. When the pain became unbearable, he knew that he couldn't put off [use a form of *visit*] _____ a doctor.

20. Ellen decided that Joanna was worthy _____ her trust.

66 Precise Expression II: Exactness

Good writers get into the habit of seeking out the exact word required. They avoid catchall words that can mean anything or nothing or words that fail to convey precisely the meaning of what they wish to say.

Inexact   We had a *nice* afternoon at the beach.
Exact   We had an *invigorating* afternoon at the beach.

Inexact   The movie was *good*.
Exact   The movie was *a deeply moving drama about troubled adolescents*.

Inexact   Americans are *totally interested* in sex.
Exact   Americans are *preoccupied* with sex.

Inexact   Her *immaturity* may improve as she gets older.
Exact   She may *mature* as she gets older.

---

66 Exercise/USING THE EXACT EXPRESSION

Rewrite each of the sentences below, substituting a more exact expression for those in italics.

1. The *colored* sunset was dazzling.

2. My car was *totally fixed* by the mechanic.

3. The science class was *interesting*.

4. At the trial, Lisa was an *uninterested* observer.

5. Joe decided to *except* the job.

_____

6. The President had *acclaimed* that this was the Age of Space Travel.

_____

7. The *reverence* of his statements was questionable.

8. They had *a lot of fun* at the party.

_____

9. The divorce agreement was *accomplished by negotiations.*

_____

10. The saleslady *fulfilled* my order.

_____

11. After awhile, his reputation for honesty *ebbed.*

_____

12. In writing the paper, he *exposed* what he knew about the Civil War.

_____

13. Taking any kind of exam *is not easy.*

_____

14. My lawyers are *adjusting* my case against my landlord.

_____

15. He had many *allusions* about marriage.

_____

16. Unemployment was *ripe* in this part of the country.

_____

17. On the camping trip, we were *subjected* to the wonders of nature.

_____

18. He *inferred* that he wouldn't be back at school in the fall.

_____

19. She had *trouble* with her boyfriend.

_____

20. The dog knew him by his *odor*.

_____

67 Wordiness

Using more words than are necessary causes your writing to lose vigor. Clear, direct, and forceful writing requires that you use as few words as possible but as many as necessary to say what you mean. Avoid the following forms of wordiness.

Avoid Redundancy and Eliminate Deadwood

Redundancy means "needless repetition." Examine your work carefully, paying special attention to the following.

1. Wherever possible, transform your clauses into phrases and your phrases into single words. By this means, you eliminate deadwood.

Deadwood The professor, *who teaches English*, was my mentor.
Revised The professor of English was my mentor.
Revised The English professor was my mentor.

Deadwood The dress was red *in color*.
Revised The dress was red.

Deadwood After the game *had come to an end*, we drove home.
Revised After the game, we drove home.

2. Use a single exact word instead of two vague ones.

Vague a *real* and *true* friend
Better a *genuine* friend

Vague I had great *regard* and *respect* for her.
Better I *cared* for her very much.

3. Eliminate words or expressions that repeat what you have already said.

Repetitious He made *revised changes* in his book.
Revised He *made changes* in his book.

or

He *revised* his book.

Repetitious The cook *combined together* eggs and cream.
Revised The cook *combined* eggs and cream.

4. Do not use several words where one will do.

Hackneyed and Wordy	Better
In this day and age	
in the modern world	today
it should be noticed	notice
as far as _____ is concerned	(just use the noun that fits the blank)
at this point in time	now
by means of	by

Avoid Awkward Repetition

Effective repetition of words can make for vigorous emphasis; awkward repetition is merely wordy: It makes for dullness.

Awkward The *movers* began our *move* beautifully by *moving* the piano through the window.
Revised The movers began beautifully by getting the piano through the window.

Awkward We followed their *directions* and went *direct* to Maine on Route 1.
Revised We followed their directions and went to Main on Route 1.

Effective Repetition Back in my home town, there were the *same* streets, the *same* people, the *same* boredom.

You can *travel* here, *travel* there, *travel* everywhere, but you'll still be *traveling* with yourself.

Avoid Using Wordy Formulas

Eliminate from your writing such formulas as the following:

to be	there is	I believe
the fact that	it is	I think
type of	the use of	in my opinion
field of	situation	

Wordy
She seems *to be* happy today.
In my opinion, fitness is important to health.
Because *of the fact that* it was snowing, our tires were spinning.
I got the *type of* job I wanted.
It was a crisis *situation*.
His *use of* French is bad.

Read these examples by eliminating the italicized portions.

Avoid Using the Passive Voice

The active voice is less wordy and more vigorous.

Passive It was observed that homesickness is felt by many freshmen.
Active We observed that many freshmen feel homesick.

Avoid Using Complicated Diction

Use plain rather than fancy diction to avoid wordiness.

Fancy The utmost in building height has been achieved by the World Trade Center towers.
Plain The tallest buildings are the World Trade Center towers.

Fancy We were hardly able to commence the festivities considering that the presence of the guest of honor was felt as an absence.
Plain We couldn't start the party without the guest of honor.

---

67   Exercise/ELIMINATING WORDINESS

A. Rewrite the following sentences, eliminating the wordy deadwood.

1. I am preparing a short, condensed digest of my article that will serve as a précis.

   _____

   _____

2. The man who was wearing the white suit looked like my Uncle Charles.

   _____

   _____

3. As a rule, Jane would normally go to bed at her usual early hour.

   _____

   _____

4. After telling my mother the bad news, I could see that she was deeply affected by what I had told her.

_____

_____

5. When the bell had rung, we walked out of the room and left.

_____

_____

6. After walking awhile, we found that we had circled around the circumference of the camp.

_____

_____

7. I am learning the technique of how to do the work of the job.

_____

_____

8. According to the basic fundamentals of physics, a particle losing energy will eventually disappear from view.

_____

_____

9. If you combine together cake and ice cream, you'll have a wonderful dessert.

_____

_____

10. After the concert had come to an end, we drove on home.

_____

_____

B. Eliminate all wordy formulas from the following by rewriting each sentence.

1. In my opinion, the world is getting crazier every day.

   _____

   _____

2. Another aspect of the situation that needs to be examined is mass transportation.

   _____

   _____

3. She appears to be happy with a crisis situation.

   _____

   _____

4. I have the type of stereo I have always wanted.

   _____

   _____

5. Because of the fact that it's now 2 o'clock a.m. in the morning in Paris, we'd better not phone Pierre.

   _____

   _____

6. The field of biophysics is growing.

   _____

   _____

7. It is a fact that many people watch television too much.

   _____

   _____

8. There are many reasons why crime is on the increase.

_____

_____

9. I believe my mother always believed in women's liberation.

_____

_____

10. She appeared to be dissatisfied with her new job.

_____

_____

C. Correct the following sentences, which contain various wordiness errors.

1. The race ended in a dead heat and a tie, three cars finishing at exactly the same time.

_____

_____

2. In this modern world, nations achieve national status by means of internal revolution.

_____

_____

3. It was thought that loneliness is felt by many freshmen.

_____

_____

4. In a few words, she gave a short summary of the committee's report.

_____

_____

5. The driver drove steadily over the treacherous and dangerous highway; his driving made us feel safe.

_____

_____

6. Let's refer back to page 12.

_____

_____

7. The extraordinary size of the sum of money he advanced to me from his personal funds was a gesture that went beyond mere kind generosity.

_____

_____

8. The edifice was entirely and totally consumed by the conflagration.

_____

_____

9. His face was red in color.

_____

_____

10. When the time came to leave, Joyce left.

_____

_____

68 Slang and Nonstandard English

Slang can be vigorous, colorful, and racy; in fact, when adopted for formal use, slang adds a kind of refreshing zest to language. But all too often slang words are known only to a small group and have no meaning to the rest of us. Like slang and widely used in conversation, nonstandard English constructions are known only to a small part of the public and are thus inappropriate for formal writing assignments. Nonstandard English, moreover, announces an uneducated provincialism. Neither slang nor nonstandard English, therefore, is useful for wide-ranging communication. Both should be avoided, unless, as in the case of slang, a particular construction has gained widespread currency. The dictionary is the place to check for appropriateness.

Slang I didn't want to cop out on the course, so I asked the prof what was going down while I was sick.
Formal I didn't want to fall behind in my work, so I asked the professor what had been happening in the course while I was sick.
Nonstandard They was tellin themself not to give nothing to nobody.
Standard They were telling themselves not to give anything to anybody.

68 Exercise/CORRECTING SLANG AND NONSTANDARD ENGLISH

Rewrite the following sentences, substituting standard English for any slang and nonstandard English constructions you find. If any are correct, place the letter C in the space provided.

> *Example* Ever since I left college, I've been going through the changes.
>
> Ever since I left college, my attitudes have been changing.

1. The soul brother's house was ripped off last night.

2. I ain't jive'n you, man; Nelson is really spaced out.

_____

_____

3. That party was a very spooky scene.

_____

_____

4. Americans are hung up on nostalgia.

_____

_____

5. Where is the English office at?

_____

_____

6. Marsha's such a sucker you could sell her the Brooklyn Bridge.

_____

_____

7. I won't never leave you go to the movies with me again.

_____

_____

8. I really get off on old Beatles' records.

_____

_____

9. Being that he didn't eat all day, he was good and hungry.

_____

_____

10. My daughter is a high school dropout.

_____

_____

11. My analyzation show that this dude is the villain.

_____

_____

12. He is like dopey anyways.

_____

_____

13. Teenyboppers freak out over Fleetwood Mac.

_____

_____

14. They was considerable upset when they seed the bill for the dinner.

_____

_____

15. She could of been alright if she'da only kept cool.

_____

_____

16. He done never knowed what hit him.

_____

_____

17. If she won't stop bitching, we won't schlep her to the blast.

_____

_____

18. I just flashed that I was dead.

_____

_____

19. He gets real antsy around exam time.

_____

_____

20. I'm dating a real fox tonight; I hope I don't flip out when I pick her up.

_____

_____

69 Clichés

A *cliché* is a trite or worn-out expression. That is, a cliché is an expression, a word, or a phrase, whose clarity and freshness have been lost through constant usage. Clichés should be avoided, for they add nothing to a discussion and generally reveal that the writer is presenting not only tired words but tired ideas as well.

69 Exercise/AVOIDING THE USE OF CLICHÉS

Rewrite the sentences below, substituting fresh language for any clichés you find.

1. Although he looked weak, Bill was actually as strong as an ox.

   _____

   _____

2. Adolescents can eat you out of house and home.

   _____

   _____

3. My Aunt Jackie was sick as a dog yesterday.

   _____

   _____

4. On balance, I think the new law is a good one.

   _____

   _____

5. It's a crying shame that Jim had his car stolen.

_____

_____

6. Dooley really has to be brought back to reality.

_____

_____

7. With his new job, Eddie is moving up the ladder of success.

_____

_____

8. In a tense situation, Joel is as cool as a cucumber.

_____

_____

9. In today's world, nations cannot afford to get hot under the collar.

_____

_____

10. When the going gets rough and it's pitch-black outside and raining cats and dogs, it's nice to know that Maggie will be the rock of Gibraltar.

_____

_____

11. Lila is pretty as a picture and neat as a pin.

_____

_____

12. Olivia has a deep, dark secret.

_____

_____

13. Last but not least, may I present my brother-in-law?

_____

_____

14. I have a sneaking suspicion that he was born with a silver spoon in his mouth.

_____

_____

15. Now that he's gone through the operation he's sadder but wiser.

_____

_____

16. To add insult to injury, she deserted me in my hour of need.

_____

_____

17. If you took him out of the classroom, he'd be like a fish out of water.

_____

_____

18. I just think he's rotten to the core.

_____

_____

19. The trouble with him is that he can't face the music.

_____

_____

20. What I like about the mayor is that he tells it like it is.

_____

_____

70   Exercise/REVIEW TEST: DICTION

A. Distinguish between each member of the following word groups by writing sentences using each word correctly.

1. infrequent, uncommon, scarce, rare

_____

_____

_____

_____

_____

_____

_____

2. perform, execute, discharge, accomplish

_____

_____

_____

_____

_____

_____

_____

3. ensure, insure, assure, secure

_____

_____

_____

_____

_____

_____

B. The sentences below are filled with slang, clichés, and nonstandard English expressions. Correct them, using fresh, standard English.

1. She left no stone unturned in her search for a job.

_____

_____

2. Emptying the refrigerator, they really pigged out over the weekend.

_____

_____

3. I ain't goin to get into no hassle with you, man.

_____

_____

4. Little girls are as sweet as sugar.

_____

_____

5. He have no right to be tellin me what to do.

_____

_____

6. You having a lot of trouble turning over that turkey.

_____

_____

7. No matter how critical the situation, I always stay calm, cool, and collected.

_____

_____

8. That was a real funky little movie.

_____

_____

9. I can get behind your philosophy.

_____

_____

10. We do be grooving at the disco tonight.

_____

_____

C. The following sentences should be rewritten to correct nonidiomatic expressions and replace vague and general language.

1. There's a tree in the middle of the grass.

_____

_____

2. Let's have some meat tonight.

_____

_____

3. I'm bored of this movie. Let's leave. Anything is preferable against this.

_____

_____

4. I can't help but to go shopping for new clothes.

_____

_____

5. She's really nice and her brother is really nice, too.

_____

_____

6. *Gorky Park* was a really good book. I enjoyed it.

_____

_____

7. The documentary on Lincoln was very interesting.

_____

_____

8. I live in the country.

_____

_____

9. The Dean should refrain of further interference.

_____

_____

10. George was ashamed at his conduct.

_____

_____

    D. These sentences are far too wordy. Rewrite each, getting rid of what is unnecessary.

1. His movement of the wheel set the wheel in motion.

_____

_____

2. The owner of the store told us the merchandise was a bummer.

_____

_____

3. Al was a warm and friendly personal friend.

_____

_____

4. She is beautiful in appearance but she is not an intelligent kind of person.

_____

_____

5. As far as economics is concerned, it is a difficult course.

_____

_____

6. It should be noticed that spring is just around the corner.

_____

_____

7. At this point in time, I need money for tuition.

_____

_____

8. Two methods of computation are shown in the diagrams in the book.

_____

_____

9. It was voted by the town council that no cars may be parked in the square.

_____

_____

10. In my opinion, he got the type of job he wanted through the use of aggressive action.

_____

_____

Spelling

PART

8

Spelling

71 Spelling I: Rules and Notes

If you are reading this section, you obviously regard yourself as a poor speller. Cheer up. All spelling is a habit and habits can be *changed*—with disciplined work.

1. Be aware when you are in doubt about the spelling of a word. Don't shrug it off. If you're in doubt, you can eliminate the doubt by learning the correct spelling. If you're not in doubt, you'll continue to make the error.
2. When you've found the correct spelling of a word, don't try to memorize it. It won't work. You must drill yourself. Try this: Look carefully at the offending word, syllable by syllable. Close your eyes and try to visualize how it looks—the order of its letters. If you can't, look at it some more. When you've managed to visualize it, try writing it out—correctly spelled. Once you've been able to do this three times, use the word in a sentence three more times. If you should fail at some stage, go back to an earlier stage of the drill.
3. Keep tabs on the words you misspell; make a list and keep it handy. Notice if there are particular kinds of words you consistently misspell and locate the rule below that you violate. Go over it carefully.
4. Don't reserve certain words for writing and some for speaking. Pronouncing all the words you know is an aid to spelling and to building vocabulary.
5. Proofread everything you write at least once for spelling errors alone.
6. Develop methods of your own to help you in your particular problem. Some people use flash cards; others use quizzes made up by friends. There are numerous possibilities.

Developing into a competent speller is important for any number of reasons: most employers who engage the services of professionals require that they write standard English correctly spelled. Maybe more important is that most readers think of poor spelling as a sure sign of incompetent, perhaps ignorant, writing; most readers think these things despite the fact that they are not necessarily true.

The following rules and notes will help you with your spelling problems.

Rule 1: *ie* and *ei*

This jingle is famous:

i before *e*
except after *c*
or when sounded like *a*
as in *neighbor* and *weigh*.

i before *e*	*ei* after *c*	*ei* as in *neighbor* and *weigh*
belief	ceiling	freight
fierce	conceive	veil
wield	receipt	skein
exceptions	exceptions	exceptions
either	financier	sleight
neither	species	height
seizure		eider
sheik		
leisure		
weird		

Rule 2: Final Silent *-e*

1. Final silent *e* is usually dropped before adding a suffix that begins with a vowel.

argue—arguing	dare—daring	baste—basting
give—giving	charge—charging	assure—assuring

2. Final silent *e* is usually retained when adding a suffix that begins with a consonant.

arrange—arrangement	love—lovely
sure—surely	hate—hateful
like—likeness	sore—soreness

Exceptions

1. Final silent *e* is retained after soft *c* (as in *dance*—as opposed to hard *c*, as in *color*) and soft *g* (*rage*—as opposed to *glove*) when adding suffixes beginning with *a* or *o*. Because *c* and *g* are generally hard before *a*, *o*, and *u*, we keep the silent *e* in order to keep the consonant soft.

charge—charging—chargeable
stage—staging—stageable
slice—slicing—sliceable

330

2. In some words, the final silent *e* must be retained before the suffix *-ing* in order to prevent mispronunciation or ambiguity of meaning.

singe—singeing (to scorch; retains *e* to prevent confusion with *singing*)
dye—dyeing (to tint; to prevent confusion with *die—dying*)

3. Final silent *e* is retained when the suffixes *-ye, -oe,* or *-ee* precede the suffix *-ing.*

free—freeing   hoe—hoeing   see—seeing
tree—treeing   eye—eyeing   shoe—shoeing

Rule 3: Final *y*

Followed by a suffix other than one beginning with the letter *i*, final *y* is usually changed to an *i*.

marry—marriage   beauty—beautiful   busy—business

When the suffix begins with an *i*, retain final *y:*

cry—crying   enjoy—enjoying

Some exceptions: day—daily; lay—laid; pay—paid; say—said.

Rule 4: Final Consonants

A final single consonant is doubled when adding a suffix that begins with a vowel under the following conditions:

1. when it appears after a single vowel, as in *allot,* or ends a monosyllabic word, as in *bat* or *run.*
2. when it is the final consonant of a word stressed on the last syllable, as in *preFER.*

Without *both* these conditions, the consonant is not doubled.

beg—begging   ship—shipping   begin—beginning   equip—equipping
forGET—forGETTING   comPEL—comPELLING

Note 1: Noun Plurals, Third-Person Singular Verbs

1. When a noun ends in a sound that allows a pronounceable final *-s,* add *-s* to form its plural. For verbs having this capacity, add *-s* to form the third-person singular present tense.

Nouns	Verbs
stone—stones	trust—trusts
pill—pills	know—knows
drawer—drawers	love—loves

Exceptions: tomato—tomatoes; buffalo—buffaloes; echo—echoes; veto—vetoes.

2. When a noun ends in a sound that does not allow a pronounceable final *-s*, add *-es* to form its plural. For verbs without this capacity, add *-es* to form the third-person singular present tense.

Nouns	Verbs
lunch—lunches	pass—passes
tax—taxes	wish—wishes

3. To form the plural of a noun ending in *y* preceded by a consonant, change the *y* to *i* and add *-es*. For a verb with the same ending, do the same to form the third-person singular present tense.

Nouns	Verbs
company—companies	carry—carries
party—parties	fly—flies

4. When a noun ending in *y* is preceded by *a*, *e*, *o*, or *u*, form the plural by adding *-s*. For a verb with the same ending, do the same to form the third-person singular present tense.

Nouns	Verbs
day—days	buy—buys
boy—boys	pay—pays
toy—toys	enjoy—enjoys
key—keys	

5. Certain nouns borrowed from other languages frequently form their plurals by retaining the form of the original language.

alumna—alumnae
alumnus—alumni
basis—bases
datum—data
phenomenon—phenomena

However, there is a tendency to give some of these an anglicized plural, and some dictionaries list two plural forms. See the dictionary for acceptable plurals of these:

focus, index, radius, beau, stadium

Note 2: Suffixes to Preserve Hard *c*

To preserve the hard sound of *c*, words ending in that sound add a *k* before a suffix ending in *e*, *i*, or *y*.

panic—panicked—panicky
mimic—mimicked—mimicking
traffic—trafficked—trafficking

Note 3: Four Special Words and the -*eed* Sound

1. *Supersede* is the only word in the English language ending in -*sede*.

2. *Exceed*, *proceed*, and *succeed* are the only words in English ending in -*ceed*.

3. Thus all other words in English having the -*eed* sound at the end are spelled -*cede:*

accede, concede, intercede, precede, recede, secede

---

71 Exercise/SPELLING BY THE RULES

A. Complete the spelling of the following words by filling in the spaces with either *ie* or *ei*.

1. ch ____ f   6. for ____ gn

2. ____ ther   7. forf ____ t

3. c ____ ling   8. v ____ l

4. rec ____ ing   9. w ____ ghty

5. r ____ n   10. rel ____ ve

B. Which of the following are spelled correctly and which not? Place a *C* in the space after the words spelled correctly; use the space to spell correctly those that are not.

1. mischeif _____

2. sovereign _____

3. concieve _____

4. acheivment _____

5. seige _____

6. liesure _____

7. hiefer _____

8. wierd _____

9. teir _____

10. conscentious _____

    C. In the following exercise, you are given a root word and a suffix. Add the two together and write the correctly spelled result in the space to the right. With some combinations you will have to add, with some subtract, and with some change a letter.

    Examples   bat + ing = batting
                    awe + ful = awful
                    lonely + ness = loneliness

1. ship + ing _____

2. judge + ment _____

3. stop + er _____

4. run + er _____

5. hope + ing _____

6. shop + ing _____

7. recur + ence _____

8. nerve + ous _____

9. enclose + ure _____

10. allot + ing _____

11. prejudice + ial _____

12. crate + ing _____

13. refuse + al _____

14. hurry + ed _____

15. love + able _____

16. rely + ance _____

17. trace + able _____

18. stop + able _____

19. chop + ing _____

20. become + ing _____

21. bore + dom _____

22. busy + ness _____

23. pretty + ness _____

24. drag + ing _____

25. holy + ness _____

26. cram + ed _____

27. shoe + ing _____

28. care + ful _____

29. permit + ed _____

30. forget + able _____

31. omit + ed _____

32. use + age _____

33. dye + ing _____

34. die + ing _____

35. breathe + able _____

36. continue + ance _____

37. prove + able _____

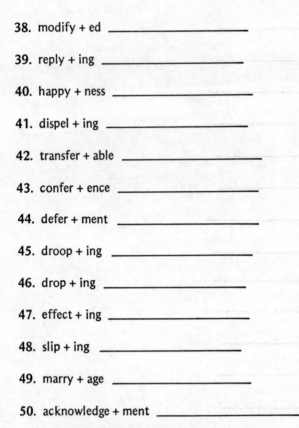

38. modify + ed _____

39. reply + ing _____

40. happy + ness _____

41. dispel + ing _____

42. transfer + able _____

43. confer + ence _____

44. defer + ment _____

45. droop + ing _____

46. drop + ing _____

47. effect + ing _____

48. slip + ing _____

49. marry + age _____

50. acknowledge + ment _____

D. Proofread the following paragraph for spelling errors. Remember: Use your doubts and your dictionary where necessary.

The man was clearly an imposter. He claimed to be the riegning monarch of another planet in our solar system, but he wasn't noticeably different than other people in Centerville. He said he's come a vast distance accross interstellar space, but he had no foriegn accent. He said the enviroment of his planet made ours seem to have less breathable air, but he looked to me as if he could breath properly. He said that what we were doing to our ecosystem was sacrilegious but I noticed him flicking ashes on the sidewalk like the other cigarete smokers. His cloths were like ours and everything about him made him look familar. Then it hit me: he was familar because he was just like us. He was incane.

72 Spelling II: Words That Sound Alike

Words that have the same pronunciation but different spellings and different meanings are called *homonyms*. They are a great cause of misspelling.

Learn to use the dictionary to distinguish between confusing homonyms.

72 Exercise/DISTINGUISHING BETWEEN HOMONYMS

Fill in the blank spaces with the correct word from the choices given in parentheses. Use your dictionary if you are not sure which to choose. When you find that your choice was either doubtful or wrong, copy the sentence again, in your notebook this time, and consult the sentence or sentences again the day after you do this exercise.

1. He took a deep (breath, breathe) _____ and said,

   "(There, They're, Their) _____ , I can (breath, breathe)

   _____ again."

2. According to (you're, your) _____ calculations, you

   should be able (to, too, two) _____ get (there, their,

   they're) _____ in about (to, too, two) _____
   hours.

3. (Who, Whose) _____ is willing to stand by and see an innocent person go to jail?

4. As a matter of (principle, principal) _____ , I never lend

   money to friends—regardless of (weather, whether) _____
   or not I have the money.

5. He had (formally, formerly) _____ been the Dean, but

   now he was Chairman of the Faculty (Council, Counsel) _____ .

6. Although he was (all ready, already) _____ in his six-

   ties, he continued to be (quiet, quite) _____ firm in his
   determination to remarry and raise another family.

7. Because the car was completely wrecked, it was (all together, altogether)

   _____ necessary to get to the (capitol, capital)

   _____ by some alternate means of transportation.

8. That he was suddenly rich did not (altar, alter) _____

   his decision to build a home on a (desert, dessert) _____

   (isle, aisle) _____ .

9. We had (passed, past) _____ the point of no return

   (weather, whether) _____ we liked it or not.

10. We thought we should stay (awhile, a while) _____ , but

    our host seemed fidgety; (there, their, they're) _____

    were signs that we (where, were) _____ having a dis-

    quieting (affect, effect) _____ on him.

11. The (effect, affect) _____ your love has had on me is to

    make me (accept, except) _____ myself in a more posi-
    tive way.

12. You (to, too, two) _____ can be poor rather (then,

    than) _____ rich; all you need to do is spend money as I
    do.

13. He can't seem to (bear, bare) _____ his soul to his psy-

    chiatrist; he's (all together, altogether) _____ (to, too,

two) _____ shy, for when he tries, a sense of great

shame (envelops, envelopes) _____ him.

14. (Any way, Anyway) _____ they chose to travel to New

York would (assure, insure) _____ that they would see
New Jersey.

15. (Your, You're) _____ much more likely to give me

good (advice, advise) _____ than he is.

16. The movie (who's, whose) _____ major subject is sex

will most likely be (band, banned) _____ in Boston.

17. It doesn't matter (where, were) _____ you buy (your,

you're) _____ shoes, as long as they fit well.

18. Walking down the (aisle, isle) _____ is not necessarily

(capital, capitol) _____ punishment; (its, it's)

_____ a loving commitment.

19. The cat made the (assent, ascent) _____ up the side of

the roof, stopping once in (a while, awhile) _____ to

lick (it's, its) _____ paws.

20. Her education served a (dual, duel) _____ purpose: it

would make her (all ready, already) _____ for graduate

school and it would enable her to live her life (any way, anyway)

_____ she wanted.

73 Diagnostic Pretest

The test you are about to take has been designed to evaluate your performance, before the course begins, in the areas of I. Recognizing Whole Sentences, II. Recognizing Basic Sentence Faults, III. Internal Punctuation, IV. Diction and Exactness in Sentences, V. Paragraphs, VI. Spelling, and VII. Mechanics. There are sixty multiple-choice items that you will be expected to finish in approximately fifty minutes.

An answer sheet appears immediately after the test. Be sure to darken the appropriate spaces. If you should omit an item anywhere along the way, be sure to skip the item number on your answer sheet, otherwise, a whole string of your answers could be marked wrong.

Your instructor will discuss with you the significance of your test score.

I. Recognizing Whole Sentences

Each numbered word group in the paragraph given below is correctly described by one of the following notations.

1. Run-on or fused sentence.
2. Comma splice or comma fault.
3. Sentence fragment.
4. Correct whole sentence.

Mark your answer sheet appropriately for each item and then correct the sentences that need correcting.

Example   Our family was very poor/. I remember many nights when supper was bread and beans.

¹Our passionate interest in sports is an interest in play and an interest in competition, both things go together. ²Although we make a fetish of winning. ³Which is not a bad thing. ⁴We are really involved in testing ourselves we like the

idea of surpassing ourselves in physical prowess and tactical shrewdness. [5] When Americans play around, it's a serious business.

II. Recognizing Basic Sentence Faults

Some of the following sentences contain errors in standard English, which is the language of educated journalism, serious magazine articles, and the like. Some are correct. Each sentence may be described with one of the following:

1. Error in subject-verb agreement.
2. Error in pronoun use: erroneous or ambiguous.
3. Error in verb form.
4. Sentence is correct.

After you have marked your answer sheet, correct the errors you have found.

Example   George is a wonderful piano player; he learned ~~it~~ ^to play^ as a young-ster.

6. Nobody has received their preregistration forms yet.
7. If one is to keep healthy and fit, you must allow time for regular exercise.
8. None of these radios cost more than fifteen dollars.
9. The truck, as well as the bus, was ignoring the speed limit.
10. If they would have woken up earlier, they would have been able to get breakfast in the dining room.
11. He should of studied harder for the exam.
12. My mother gave my sister and me identical bracelets for Christmas.
13. In many corporate financial reports, they give projected earnings for the next five years.
14. His politics is slightly to the right of center.
15. Neither his aunt nor his uncles plays golf.
16. Arthur and him were very rich men.
17. Is the dealer preparation and sales tax included in the price you quoted me?
18. When the doorbell rings, either James or Bobby go to answer it.

19. Maggie reminded Emily that her slip was showing.

20. He wanted to build up his physique so that he could make the football team. That was hard.

III. Internal Punctuation

Some of the following sentences need internal punctuation. Some are correct as they are. Decide which of the following descriptions fits the sentence and mark your answer sheet accordingly.

1. Sentence needs a comma/commas.
2. Sentence needs a semicolon.
3. Sentence needs a colon.
4. Sentence is correct.

   Examples

   Stephen, who was James's best friend, lived downtown.

<table>
<tr><td>1</td><td>2</td><td>3</td><td>4</td></tr>
<tr><td>■</td><td>□</td><td>□</td><td>□</td></tr>
</table>

   He had no money and no prospects; however, he had his health and that was important.

<table>
<tr><td>1</td><td>2</td><td>3</td><td>4</td></tr>
<tr><td>□</td><td>■</td><td>□</td><td>□</td></tr>
</table>

After you have marked your answer sheet, insert the correct punctuation where needed.

21. My doctor who goes on vacation in August leads a busy professional life.

22. To make a camping trip a success, you had better take along the following: good bedding, adequate food, and protection against insects.

23. The pianist was passionate powerful and eminently musical.

24. The colonel who came from Mississippi, served his country in two world conflagrations.

25. She had a rather high and delicate soprano however, she controlled her voice beautifully.

26. Although they arrived at the concert early they found it was sold out.

27. His grades were only average nevertheless, he was accepted into medical school.

342

28. There are only three reasons to own a car you have no public transportation to rely on, you're hungry for power and need that engine under your control, you're a masochist and enjoy the pain of keep it in working order.
29. The man leaning over the railing is my English professor.
30. After the horse ate the man strolled down to the track.
31. She wore a short gray dress.
32. All I need after graduation are graduation gifts, job offers a vacation and an apartment.
33. She was interested in physics, so she decided to major in engineering.
34. The audience which came to jeer stayed to applaud.
35. Frequently large doses of aspirin will cure a cold.

IV. Diction and Exactness in Sentences

A. Clarity and Directness

One sentence in each of the following groups of four is clearer and more direct than the others in expressing the same idea. Mark your answer sheet with your selections.

Example

1. Some people take their vacations in the winter of the year and this they definitely think is best.
2. Winter vacationing seems the best thing to some people.
3. Some people prefer to take their vacations in the winter.
4. Every winter, vacations are taken by some people who are convinced that their choice is the best one.

```
        1   2   3   4
        □   □   ■   □
```

36. 1. For eight years now, a modest little Chevy Vega, which is the car I am discussing, has served me very well.
    2. A modest little Chevy Vega, mine for eight years, which is a fair amount of time, has served me very well all that time.
    3. My car, which is a modest little Chevy Vega, has served me well for eight years.
    4. My car, a modest little Chevy Vega, has served me well for eight years.
37. 1. In today's world, which we all know is highly technological, no one should be so uneducated as to be without a working knowledge of the computer.
    2. To be without a working knowledge of the computer in the technological world of this day and age—well, none should be without it.

3. In this technological age, no one should be without a working knowledge of the computer.
4. The computer is so important to this advanced age of technology that no one should ever be without a real knowledge of the computer.

38. 1. A professional complainer is when you never have enough to be sufficient.
2. A professional complainer is someone for whom enough is never sufficient.
3. To be a professional complainer is to be the kind of a person whose idea of sufficient is never enough.
4. Sufficient is never the proper amount, never good enough for the professional complainer.

39. 1. Really uptight and steaming because the people in the courtroom were pretty wild, the judge suddenly told the bailiff to get the people out because they wouldn't cool it.
2. The spectators' outbursts having made the judge furious and annoyed, the judge proceeded to order everyone to split.
3. Angry and frustrated by the spectators' outbursts, the judge abruptly ordered the courtroom cleared.
4. The judge, angry and very frustrated by the continuous racket made by the spectators, abruptly ordered the courtroom cleared.

40. 1. She was clever enough and confident enough as a candidate for law school to meet the challenge of difficult study.
2. For law school, she was clever enough and confident enough as a candidate to take on difficult study without any problem at all.
3. Confident enough and clever enough, she, as a candidate for law school, could meet the challenge of difficult study.
4. As a candidate for law school, she was clever enough and confident enough to meet the challenge of difficult study.

41. 1. A superb teacher with a passionate interest in his subject and his students, he has a lightning quick capacity to make analogies that illuminate his ideas.
2. He can make analogies that illuminate his ideas with lightning speed because he is a superb teacher with a passionate interest in his students and his subject.
3. Lightning quick with analogies that illuminate his ideas, he is a superb teacher with a passionate interest in his subject and his students.
4. He is a superb teacher with a passionate interest in his subject and his students and a lightning quick capacity to make analogies that illuminate his ideas.

B. Subordination

The following items consist of related short sentences followed by four possible reworkings of the material. Select the one reworking that does the clearest and most logical job of subordinating and/or coordinating the short sentences. Mark your answer sheet accordingly.

Example

There's a movie festival at the Union. Three westerns, several horror movies, and a love story are on the program. There is also an odd little number about a kid looking for his mother.

1. On the program of the movie festival at the Union are three westerns, several horror movies, and a love story, along with an odd little number about a kid looking for his mother.
2. Along with an odd little number about a kid looking for his mother, the movie festival program at the Union includes three westerns, several horror movies, and a love story.
3. Among the westerns, horror movies, and love story featured on the program of the Union film festival is an odd little number about a kid looking for his mother.
4. The features in the Union film festival include three westerns, several horror movies, a love story, and an odd little number about a kid looking for his mother.

      1   2   3   4

      ☐   ☐   ☐   ■

42. America is rich. We have mineral resources. We have heavy and light manufacturing. We have a vast agriculture. Still, many individuals are feeling the pinch. They don't see themselves as rich and prosperous.

1. America is rich in mineral resources, manufacturing, and agriculture and many individuals are feeling the pinch and don't see themselves as rich and prosperous.
2. Many individuals are feeling the pinch and don't see themselves as rich and prosperous, while America is rich in mineral resources, manufacturing, and agriculture.
3. Although America is rich in mineral resources, manufacturing, and agriculture, many individuals are feeling the pinch and don't see themselves as rich and prosperous.
4. Because America is rich in mineral resources, manufacturing, and agriculture, many individuals are feeling the pinch and don't see themselves as rich and prosperous.

43. The Yankees are a professional baseball team. They were owned by CBS. CBS was conservative. The team was doing badly. George Steinbrenner, an aggressive businessman, bought the team. He spent money to get quality players. The team is now winning.

1. When the baseball Yankees were owned by CBS, a conservative company, they did badly, but when they were bought by George Steinbrenner, an aggressive businessman who spent money to get quality players, they started to win.
2. CBS, a conservative company owned the baseball Yankees and under CBS, they did poorly until George Steinbrenner, an aggressive businessman, bought them and spent the money to get quality players who could win.
3. CBS, a conservative company, owners of the baseball Yankees before George Steinbrenner an aggressive businessman bought them, did poorly with the team but Steinbrenner did well because he spent the money to get quality players who won for him.
4. Owned by CBS, a conservative company, the baseball Yankees did poorly, but owned by George Steinbrenner, an aggressive businessman who spent money for quality players, they are winning.

44. *Jaws* was a best-seller. It was written by Peter Benchley. It was a best-seller for more than a year. Then it was made into a movie. The movie was directed by Steven Spielberg. The critics loved it. The public loved it better.

1. Even more than the critics, the public loved *Jaws*, the best-seller for more than a year by Peter Benchley made into a movie directed by Steven Spielberg.
2. Steven Spielberg directed the movie *Jaws* from the best-seller for more than a year by Peter Benchley which the critics loved but the public loved even better.
3. Peter Benchley was the author of *Jaws*, the best-seller made into a movie for a year, directed by Steven Spielberg, which the critics loved but the public loved even better.
4. Peter Benchley's *Jaws*, a best-seller for more than a year, was made into a movie, which the critics loved but the public loved even better, directed by Steven Spielberg.

C. Parallel Structure

From the statements given for each item, select the one that most successfully completes the item through the maintenance of parallel structure. Mark the appropriate space on your answer sheet.

Example

On his vacation, Allan liked to swim,

1. to play with his children, and to take long walks with his wife.
2. playing with his children, and take long walks with his wife.
3. and he liked playing with his children and then also go on long walks with his wife.

4. but he also liked playing with his children and he liked to go on long walks with his wife.

1   2   3   4
■   ☐   ☐   ☐

45. In order to help us with our math problems, the professor suggested

1. longer study periods, review of elementary algebra, and that we go to the tutorial center.
2. study periods for a longer time, elementary algebra be reviewed, and that the tutorial center be visited.
3. longer study periods, review of elementary algebra, and visits to the tutorial center.
4. that study periods be longer, that we review our elementary algebra, and going to the tutorial center.

46. Martha is very intelligent,

1. has good manners, and wonderfully witty.
2. well-mannered, and wonderfully witty.
3. with good manners, and wonderfully witty.
4. well-mannered, and is wonderfully witty.

V. Paragraphs

A. Unity and Coherence

Numbers 47 and 48 refer to a set of sentences (marked 1-5) following one marked "topic sentence." If the irrelevant sentence or sentences were deleted and the others placed in an appropriate order, the set would make a unified and coherent paragraph. Your task is to make a unified and coherent paragraph so that you can correctly answer questions 47 and 48. Mark your answer sheet according to the following key:

1. Sentence 1.
2. Sentence 2.
3. Sentence 3.
4. Sentence 4.
5. Sentence 5.

Example

Topic Sentence: The Chinese suspicion of foreigners stems from a number of causes.

1. The Chinese don't mind foreigners in their restaurants.
2. China has been subjected to numerous foreign invasions and long periods of oppressive foreign domination.
3. The country is vast but essentially rural, so that clannish small settlements have always been the rule and have thus always distrusted even other Chinese from another village.
4. Chinese culture is proud; it thinks of itself as superior and fears the dilution that foreign presences can visit on any culture.
5. The Chinese family is close-knit and, while hospitable enough to strangers, rarely gives them its full confidence.

Which sentence violates the unity of the paragraph?

```
1   2   3   4   5
■   □   □   □   □
```

Topic Sentence: A woman's financial independence is as crucial to her as a man's is to him.

1. Dependent individuals, even wives who have primary responsibility for child-rearing, are neither free nor creative and tend to impede the family's growth and development.
2. Marrying somebody wealthy is no solution.
3. Financial independence, in the form of a remunerative job or profession, is a crucial aspect of psychological independence.
4. Both sexes must have the sense of wholeness and integrity that comes with the knowledge that they are self-sustaining and thus no longer children who must be fed.
5. Psychological independence is gained in the same way by both sexes.

47. Which sentence should come immediately after the topic sentence?
48. Which sentence violates the unity of the paragraph?

B. Paragraph Development

Numbers 49 and 50 are topic sentences whose content suggests a specific type of paragraph development. Choose the most appropriate one for each topic sentence by marking your answer sheet with one of the following methods of development.

1. Illustrative details
2. Comparison and contrast
3. Definition
4. Classification
5. Causal analysis

   Example   There are four types of professor on this campus.

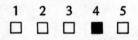

```
1   2   3   4   5
□   □   □   ■   □
```

348

49. The new diesel-engined cars are more economical to run than the old gasoline-engined cars.
50. If we examine the criminal's life, we can see the genesis of crime.

VI. Spelling

In each of the sets of words given below, one is incorrectly spelled. Indicate which word that is by darkening the appropriate space on your answer sheet. Then add and/or subtract the letters that would leave the word correctly spelled.

Example   obedience   atrophy   dries   seperate   niece

1	2	3	4	5
□	□	□	■	□

51. judgment   cieling   cries   dissatisfy   persuade
52. studyous   frenetic   piece   occur   ingenious
53. conference   preferrence   tomato   skipping   allotment
54. hopeing   running   deference   debatable   joyous

VII. Mechanics: Capital Letters, Apostrophe, Quotation Marks

Some of the sentences given below contain errors in capitalization, the use of the apostrophe, or the use of quotation marks. Some are correct. Describe each sentence by marking your answer sheet with one of the following.

1. Error in the use of capital letters.
2. Error in the use of the apostrophe.
3. Error in the use of quotation marks.
4. Sentence is correct.

After you have marked the answer sheet, make the correction in the sentence.

Example   He answered, "I attended Fordham University."

1	2	3	4
□	□	■	□

55. Mens' hats are on sale today.
56. The Ambassador from Turkey noted that "every country has the right to protect it's territorial integrity."

57. He wrote a letter of protest to sen. Kirby.
58. We went together to see the new pottery on exhibition in Judys workshop.
59. The united nations is our sole hope for peace.
60. My daughters' vacations coincide.

73 PRETEST ANSWER SHEET

	1	2	3	4	5			1	2	3	4	5
1.	☐	☐	☐	☐	☐		31.	☐	☐	☐	☐	☐
2.	☐	☐	☐	☐	☐		32.	☐	☐	☐	☐	☐
3.	☐	☐	☐	☐	☐		33.	☐	☐	☐	☐	☐
4.	☐	☐	☐	☐	☐		34.	☐	☐	☐	☐	☐
5.	☐	☐	☐	☐	☐		35.	☐	☐	☐	☐	☐
6.	☐	☐	☐	☐	☐		36.	☐	☐	☐	☐	☐
7.	☐	☐	☐	☐	☐		37.	☐	☐	☐	☐	☐
8.	☐	☐	☐	☐	☐		38.	☐	☐	☐	☐	☐
9.	☐	☐	☐	☐	☐		39.	☐	☐	☐	☐	☐
10.	☐	☐	☐	☐	☐		40.	☐	☐	☐	☐	☐
11.	☐	☐	☐	☐	☐		41.	☐	☐	☐	☐	☐
12.	☐	☐	☐	☐	☐		42.	☐	☐	☐	☐	☐
13.	☐	☐	☐	☐	☐		43.	☐	☐	☐	☐	☐
14.	☐	☐	☐	☐	☐		44.	☐	☐	☐	☐	☐
15.	☐	☐	☐	☐	☐		45.	☐	☐	☐	☐	☐
16.	☐	☐	☐	☐	☐		46.	☐	☐	☐	☐	☐
17.	☐	☐	☐	☐	☐		47.	☐	☐	☐	☐	☐
18.	☐	☐	☐	☐	☐		48.	☐	☐	☐	☐	☐
19.	☐	☐	☐	☐	☐		49.	☐	☐	☐	☐	☐
20.	☐	☐	☐	☐	☐		50.	☐	☐	☐	☐	☐
21.	☐	☐	☐	☐	☐		51.	☐	☐	☐	☐	☐
22.	☐	☐	☐	☐	☐		52.	☐	☐	☐	☐	☐
23.	☐	☐	☐	☐	☐		53.	☐	☐	☐	☐	☐
24.	☐	☐	☐	☐	☐		54.	☐	☐	☐	☐	☐
25.	☐	☐	☐	☐	☐		55.	☐	☐	☐	☐	☐
26.	☐	☐	☐	☐	☐		56.	☐	☐	☐	☐	☐
27.	☐	☐	☐	☐	☐		57.	☐	☐	☐	☐	☐
28.	☐	☐	☐	☐	☐		58.	☐	☐	☐	☐	☐
29.	☐	☐	☐	☐	☐		59.	☐	☐	☐	☐	☐
30.	☐	☐	☐	☐	☐		60.	☐	☐	☐	☐	☐

74 Diagnostic Posttest

The test you are about to take has been designed to test your performance in the same areas as the Pretest. There are sixty multiple choice items that you will be expected to complete in approximately fifty minutes.

An answer sheet appears immediately after the test. Be sure to darken the appropriate spaces. If you should omit an item anywhere along the way, be sure to follow suit on your answer sheet; otherwise, a whole string of your answers could be marked wrong.

Your instructor will discuss with you the significance of your test score.

I. Paragraphs

A. Unity and Coherence

Questions 1 and 2 refer to a set of sentences (marked 1–5) following one marked "topic sentence." If the irrelevant sentences or sentences among 1–5 were deleted and the others placed in an appropriate order, the whole set would make a unified and coherent paragraph. Your task is to make the material into such a paragraph so that you correctly answer questions 1 and 2. Mark your answer sheet according to the following key:

1. Sentence 1.
2. Sentence 2.
3. Sentence 3.
4. Sentence 4.
5. Sentence 5.

Example

Topic Sentence: Americans are showing a clear preference for living in the so-called "Sun Belt."

1. Increasingly over the last twenty years, opportunities for employment have decreased as industry has either left the older, urban parts of the country or become obsolete.

352

2. The American West has always symbolized breaking new ground.
3. This fact is borne out by the statistics showing increasing numbers leaving the Northeast and the Midwest to settle in Florida, Texas, California, and Arizona.
4. New industries like the electronics and aerospace conglomerates have sprung up in the new parts of the United States and have attracted there people from the old.
5. No doubt fine weather in the Sun Belt has something to do with it, but this is not the only factor in people's decisions to go with the sun.

Which sentence should follow immediately after the topic sentence?

```
1   2   3   4   5
□   □   ■   □   □
```

Topic Sentence: An increasing prevalent form of housing is the cooperative apartment.

1. Because they own these shares, tenants are given leases to the apartments they will occupy.
2. Some tenants are less cooperative than others.
3. A co-op apartment building is one that is owned by the tenants who hold shares in an owner's corporation.
4. The price of co-op apartments varies from locale to locale and from building to building, but it is similar to the price of a house in the suburbs.
5. Tenants buy shares in the corporation, the number usually depending upon the size of the apartment they wish to occupy, and pay a monthly maintenance fee besides.

1. Which sentence violates the unity of the paragraph?
2. Which sentence should be the last one?

B. Paragraph Development

Questions 3 and 4 are topic sentences whose content suggests a specific type of paragraph development. Choose the most appropriate one for each topic sentence by marking your answer sheet with one of the following methods of development.

1. Illustrative details.
2. Comparison and contrast.
3. Definition.
4. Classification.
5. Causal analysis.

Example　　Consider the *crank* on the one hand and the *eccentric* on the other.

1	2	3	4	5
☐	■	☐	☐	☐

3. The concept of honesty changes from generation to generation.
4. The United Nations has been ineffective in stopping wars.

II. Diction and Exactness in Sentences

A. Clarity and Directness

One sentence in each of the following groups of four is clearer and more direct than the others in expressing the same general idea. Mark your answer sheet with your selections.

Example

1. Health experts have warned Americans that they had better reform so now you see everybody running for his or her life like mad.
2. Everybody in America is running for his or her life furiously because all the health experts have warned us that we'll be in bad health if we don't.
3. Running for our lives—that's what us Americans have been doing ever since our health experts have told us to jog or else.
4. Warned by their health experts that they had better reform, Americans are now running for their lives.

1	2	3	4
☐	☐	☐	■

5. 1. A sore loser is where you can't even remember that the score went against you.
2. A player who can't believe he lost and keeps arguing and getting mad is quite a sore loser.
3. A sore loser is a player who can't remember the score.
4. If the score goes against you in the game and you think you won, you're a sore loser.

6 1. Once upon a time in the United States, farms were owned by families who handed them down to children, but nowadays they're owned by big business, mostly.
2. Farms used to be owned by families who gave them to their children to work, but the big businesses have taken them over.
3. Big businesses own farms in the United States, while in the old days these farms were strictly owned by families who passed them down from generation to generation.

354

4. Farming in America, once a family enterprise, is now almost wholly in the hands of big business.
7. 1. Snowmobiles have ruined everything, shattering the perfect peace of snowy winter in the woods and that's why I hate the snowmobile.
   2. If it weren't for the snowmobiles that are so noisy, I could enjoy the perfect stillness of snowy woods in the winter and for that I could hate them.
   3. I hate the advent of the snowmobile because it has shattered the perfect serenity of white winters in the woods.
   4. There are no more snowy, white winters in the woods these days, ever since the coming of the snowmobile which makes such a racket.
8. 1. The medical schools have so many applicants that they can't accept them all, so when he mailed his transcripts in too late they said never mind.
   2. He was very late mailing in his transcripts to the medical school, so they ignored his application because they really get swamped with applications and one more or less doesn't make a bit of difference.
   3. Because he had mailed his transcripts in too late, the medical school, which always has more applicants than it can accept, ignored his application.
   4. Many applicants who mail their transcripts in on time never get accepted, so when his transcript came late, the medical school just decided to ignore it.
9. 1. For six years, without the slightest regret, Dr. Grimshaw had spent his every waking hour working to become a board-certified internist.
   2. To become a board-certified internist, Dr. Grimshaw, without the slightest regret for six years, spent his every waking hour.
   3. In order to become a board-certified internist without the slightest regret, Dr. Grimshaw had spent his every waking hour working for six years.
   4. Without the slightest regret, Dr. Grimshaw had spent his every waking hour for six years studying to become a board-certified internist.
10. 1. You would be foolish to go to the wilds of a national park on a camping trip and not bring along at least a compass and a pair of dry socks.
    2. If you're on a camping trip in the wilds of a national park, don't forget to bring along a compass and a pair of dry socks.
    3. In the wilds of a national park, no one on a camping trip should be without a compass and a pair of dry socks.
    4. No one on a camping trip in the wilds of a national park should be without a compass and a pair of dry socks.

B. Subordination

The following items consist of related short sentences followed by four possible reworkings of the material. Select the one that does the clearest and most logical job of subordinating and/or coordinating the short sentences and then mark your answer sheet accordingly.

Example

They started to drive at midnight. They arrived at the beach at dawn. The beach was glorious. They couldn't stay awake to enjoy it.

1. Although they started to drive to the beach at midnight, they didn't arrive until dawn, and though the beach was glorious they couldn't stay awake to enjoy it.
2. Because they started to drive to the beach at midnight and didn't arrive there until dawn, when they found the beach glorious they couldn't stay awake to enjoy it.
3. The beach was glorious but they couldn't stay awake to enjoy it because they had started to drive there at midnight and hadn't arrived till dawn.
4. They couldn't stay awake to enjoy the beach because, although it was glorious, they had started to drive there at midnight and hadn't arrived until dawn.

1	2	3	4
■	□	□	□

11. The United States was rich and powerful. It had a good intelligence network. The embassy in Teheran was seized. The fifty-two hostages were held more than a year.

1. The embassy in Teheran was seized and the fifty-two hostages were held there in captivity more than a year even though we're a rich and powerful country and despite the fact that we had a good intelligence network.
2. Although the United States was rich and powerful and had a good intelligence network, the embassy in Teheran was seized and the fifty-two hostages held more than a year.
3. The seized embassy in Teheran and the fifty-two hostages held more than a year happened in spite of the fact that the United States was rich and powerful and had a good intelligence network.
4. A good intelligence network and the fact that the United States was rich and powerful didn't count because the embassy was seized and the fifty two hostages held more than a year.

12. We think there's a lot of television to watch now. In big cities there are about fifty channels. The cable networks are expanding rapidly. We'll have to stop sleeping to watch it all.

1. Although we now think that there's lot of television to watch, with about fifty channels available in big cities, the cable networks are expanding and we'll soon have to stop sleeping to watch it all.
2. We'll have to stop sleeping to watch all the television that will be available as the cable networks keep expanding, because we'll have more television to watch than the fifty channels available in the big cities.

3. Because the cable networks are expanding we'll have to stop sleeping in order to watch the amount of television there will be, which will be more than fifty channels now available in the big cities.
4. In the big cities there are about fifty television channels to watch, but the cable networks are expanding and we'll have to stop sleeping to watch it all.

13. Woodworking is hard. Most people think it is. They have never tried. They have never tried with the right tools. They have never tried with the right wood for the right job.

1. People who have never tried woodworking with the right tools and the right wood for the right job think it's hard.
2. Those who think woodworking is hard have never tried it, using the right tools and the right wood for the right job.
3. Using the right tools and the right wood for the right job, those who think woodworking is hard wouldn't think so anymore.
4. Not having tried using the right tools and the right wood for the right job, people think woodworking is hard.

C. Parallel Structure

Each of the following items consist of four sentences saying or trying to say approximately the same thing. Select the one that is strongest because it maintains parallel structure.

Example

1. When he was young, he was energetic, with impulsiveness and the tendency toward romanticism.
2. When he was young, he was a person with energy, impulsive, and leaning toward romanticism.
3. When he was young, he was energetic, impulsive, and romantic.
4. When he was young, he could be thought of as energetic, with impulsiveness, and as having a romantic nature.

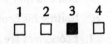

14. 1. Because he liked to be outdoors in the winter, he tried to ski, tobogganing, and to go on an ice-sailer.
2. Because he liked to be outdoors in the winter, he tried skiing, being on a toboggan, and to ice-sail.
3. Because he liked to be outdoors in the winter, he tried skiing, tobogganing, and ice-sailing.
4. Because he liked to be outdoors in the winter, he tried skis, tobogganing, and to ice-sail.

15. 1. The causes of most wars are nationalistic struggles, economic conflicts, and border disputes.
    2. The causes of most wars are nationalistic struggles, having economic conflicts with others, and disputing over borders.
    3. The causes of most wars are matters of nationalism, to gain economic advantages, and disputes over borders.
    4. The causes of most wars are nationalism, economic conficts, and border disputes.

III. Recognizing Basic Sentence Faults

Some of the following sentences contain errors in standard English, which is the language of educated journalism, serious magazine articles, and the like. Some of the sentences are correct. Each may be described with one of the following.

1. Error in subject-verb agreement.
2. Error in pronoun use: erroneous or ambiguous.
3. Error in verb form.
4. Sentence is correct.

After you have marked your answer sheet, correct the errors you have found.

Example   Allan is a wonderful photographer; he learned ~~it~~ in college.
                                                    his technique

```
1   2   3   4
☐   ■   ☐   ☐
```

16. Miriam showed Margaret that her makeup was smeared.
17. Either Linda or Bob answer the phone in their house.
18. Is the tip and sales tax included in the bill?
19. Bud and him were very knowledgeable about baseball.
20. Neither his brothers nor his sisters care for wine.
21. Economics are a little understood subject.
22. In many English composition texts, they say that diction is important.
23. My father gave my brother and me a trip to Europe for graduation.
24. He must of been asleep when I called.
25. If they would have studied harder, they would have passed math.
26. None of these cars cost more than $5,000.
27. If one is to succeed in business, you must have a fanatical dedication to hard work.

28. If anybody has their wits about them, they'll invest in oil stocks.

29. The man who drives the cars go to Florida regularly.

30. The Committee are handing down their decision today.

IV. Recognizing Whole Sentences

Each numbered word group is correctly described by one of the following notations.

1. Run-on or fused sentence.
2. Comma splice or comma fault.
3. Sentence fragment.
4. Correct whole sentence.

Mark your answer sheet appropriately and then try to correct the sentences that need correcting.

Example   My mother met my father in 1922Țĥey were married in 1924.

```
 1   2   3   4
 □   ■   □   □
```

31. On July 4 weekend, Americans celebrate.

32. Although some of us stay at home and some travel to a resort.

33. We are proud of our freedom, it was hard won.

34. In some states, fireworks are legal in others, they're not.

35. Which is an indication of American diversity.

36. Celebration symbolizes liberty.

V. Internal Punctuation

Some of the following sentences need internal punctuation. Some are correct as they are. Decide which of the following descriptions fits each sentence and mark your answer sheet accordingly.

1. Sentence needs a comma/commas.
2. Sentence needs a semicolon.
3. Sentence needs a colon.
4. Sentence is correct.

After marking your answer sheet, insert the correct punctuation where needed.

Example Bobby, who lives next door to James, is going to the Bronx Zoo today.

1	2	3	4
■	□	□	□

37. The actor, who never takes a vacation travels frequently between Hollywood and New York.
38. Woodfinishing requires the following materials: sandpaper in several grades, steel wool, turpentine, shellac, and wax polish.
39. The woods were lovely dark and deep.
40. The President who comes from California, owns a ranch with horses and cattle.
41. Small cars are very economical to run however, they frequently cost more to purchase.
42. Although she was famous she was modest.
43. Whether you're rich or poor it's always good to have money.
44. Nobody knows the troubles I've seen nevertheless, I'm sure they could sympathize with me.
45. The man, leaning against the wall, is my uncle.
46. Usually afternoons are best.
47. There are three things about camping that I hate dry food, insects, and hiking.
48. The woman wearing white is the bride.
49. After the man ate the horse followed him to the barn.
50. Helen was interested in health sciences, so she decided to try for medical school.
51. After graduation, he took a vacation found an apartment and looked for a job.

VI. Spelling

In each set of words below, one word is incorrectly spelled. Indicate which word it is by darkening the appropriate space on your answer sheet. Then add or subtract the letters that would leave the word correctly spelled.

Example   liesure   sacrilegious   pursue   torpor   recede

	1	2	3	4	5
	■	□	□	□	□

52. genius   ingenous   precious   delicious   specious
53. runing   shipping   alloting   gripping   dropping
54. personnal   quiet   science   conscience   breathing
55. proveing   priceless   believe   hypocrisy   irresistible
56. dissipated   maintainance   pastime   bachelor   transgression

VII. Mechanics

Some of the sentences given below contain errors in capitalization, the apostrophe, or quotation marks. Some are correct. Describe each sentence by marking your answer sheet with one of the following.

1. Error in the use of capital letters.
2. Error in the use of apostrophe.
3. Error in the use of quotation marks.
4. Sentence is correct.

After marking your answer sheet, correct the errors you find.

Example   She replied, "You're a terrible turkey."

	1	2	3	4
	□	□	■	□

57. The team gave it's all but it just wasn't enough.
58. The Coach told them, "Your a great bunch of athletes; some days you can be great and not win."
59. The federal bureau of investigation reported that "major crime in the United States increased by 12% in 1981."
60. He asked "if he could go to the movies with Joe."

NAME _____ DATE _____

POSTTEST ANSWER SHEET

	1	2	3	4	5			1	2	3	4	5
1.	☐	☐	☐	☐	☐		31.	☐	☐	☐	☐	☐
2.	☐	☐	☐	☐	☐		32.	☐	☐	☐	☐	☐
3.	☐	☐	☐	☐	☐		33.	☐	☐	☐	☐	☐
4.	☐	☐	☐	☐	☐		34.	☐	☐	☐	☐	☐
5.	☐	☐	☐	☐	☐		35.	☐	☐	☐	☐	☐
6.	☐	☐	☐	☐	☐		36.	☐	☐	☐	☐	☐
7.	☐	☐	☐	☐	☐		37.	☐	☐	☐	☐	☐
8.	☐	☐	☐	☐	☐		38.	☐	☐	☐	☐	☐
9.	☐	☐	☐	☐	☐		39.	☐	☐	☐	☐	☐
10.	☐	☐	☐	☐	☐		40.	☐	☐	☐	☐	☐
11.	☐	☐	☐	☐	☐		41.	☐	☐	☐	☐	☐
12.	☐	☐	☐	☐	☐		42.	☐	☐	☐	☐	☐
13.	☐	☐	☐	☐	☐		43.	☐	☐	☐	☐	☐
14.	☐	☐	☐	☐	☐		44.	☐	☐	☐	☐	☐
15.	☐	☐	☐	☐	☐		45.	☐	☐	☐	☐	☐
16.	☐	☐	☐	☐	☐		46.	☐	☐	☐	☐	☐
17.	☐	☐	☐	☐	☐		47.	☐	☐	☐	☐	☐
18.	☐	☐	☐	☐	☐		48.	☐	☐	☐	☐	☐
19.	☐	☐	☐	☐	☐		49.	☐	☐	☐	☐	☐
20.	☐	☐	☐	☐	☐		50.	☐	☐	☐	☐	☐
21.	☐	☐	☐	☐	☐		51.	☐	☐	☐	☐	☐
22.	☐	☐	☐	☐	☐		52.	☐	☐	☐	☐	☐
23.	☐	☐	☐	☐	☐		53.	☐	☐	☐	☐	☐
24.	☐	☐	☐	☐	☐		54.	☐	☐	☐	☐	☐
25.	☐	☐	☐	☐	☐		55.	☐	☐	☐	☐	☐
26.	☐	☐	☐	☐	☐		56.	☐	☐	☐	☐	☐
27.	☐	☐	☐	☐	☐		57.	☐	☐	☐	☐	☐
28.	☐	☐	☐	☐	☐		58.	☐	☐	☐	☐	☐
29.	☐	☐	☐	☐	☐		59.	☐	☐	☐	☐	☐
30.	☐	☐	☐	☐	☐		60.	☐	☐	☐	☐	☐